the*ULTIMATE*
SPORTS
handbook

Library of Congress Cataloging
in Publication Number:
2004112080

ISBN: 1-59474-034-8

Printed in Singapore

Typeset in Grotesque and
News Gothic

Designed by Bryn Ashburn

Illustrations by Michael Miller

Distributed in North America by
Chronicle Books
85 Second Street
San Francisco, CA 94105
10 9 8 7 6 5 4 3 2 1

Quirk Books
215 Church Street
Philadelphia, PA 19106
www.quirkbooks.com

the ULTIMATE
SPORTS
handbook

HOW TO
steal home,
slam dunk,
score a penalty kick,
and play like
the pros

by Richard O'Brien

foreword by Jack McCallum

QUIRK BOOKS
PHILADELPHIA

CONTENTS

PART TWO: SOLO SPORTS

PART THREE: EXTREME SPORTS

FOREWORD

One of the odious changes in my profession over the years has been the amount of time we spend chronicling events on the periphery of the games rather than the games themselves. We write about long-term contracts instead of man-to-man combat; about holdouts instead of strikeouts; about free agents instead of free safeties. Fans tell me they liked it better when sports writers stuck to sports, yet they, too, are obsessed with how much money athletes make, or whether their favorite player is going to stick around long enough to know the name of the gated community where he lives.

Once in a while, then, we need to be reminded that sports is actually about playing the game. Rich O'Brien's *The Ultimate Sports Handbook* is such a reminder. Bereft of references to conflicts between agents and management, *Handbook* provides the hows and how-tos about the fine art of—as the football coaches love to say—execution.

Among the features that distinguish *Handbook* from other instructional tomes, however, is its value for both the active athlete and the couch potato looking for vicarious thrills. It deals not only with skills you've thought about—dunking a basketball, blasting out of a sand trap, getting speed on your serve—but many you haven't. I seriously doubt that any time in the near future I'll be attempting a backflip while traveling at a high speed during a motocross race, but it's comforting that I now know at what point to "gas off" should I attempt such a maneuver. More to the point, when I watch motocross I'll have a better idea of what's going on.

Handbook is more than instruction, though; it is, in fact, a mini-history book, which isn't surprising since Rich was a history major at Yale. I learned about the "Thomas Flair" (gymnastics), the origin of the quad (figure skating), the surfing conditions on the north shore of Maui, and even a little bit more than I knew before about the sack (football). It's also that rare instruction book that sounds suspiciously like actual literature. The section on doing "the Ollie"—I'll let you discover for yourself what that is—begins with a quote from the poet Carl Sandburg. The broad canvas on which *Handbook* was written is predictable; when Rich and I worked together for five years on the "Scorecard" section at *Sports Illustrated*, I used to say we didn't need to look anything up on Google because we could just look it up on Rich.

Now you can look it up in *Handbook*. As for me, I'm off to get more spin on my serve in table tennis. I know how to do it now.

—Jack McCallum
Senior Writer
Sports Illustrated

INTRODUCTION

We are surrounded by sports. Okay, obsessed by sports. Major leagues, minor leagues; men's leagues, women's leagues. *Fantasy leagues!* Seasons overlap. March Madness rolls into spring training and right on into playoff fever. Then it's everybody into the Super Bowl pool—and don't forget to fill out your mock draft. We watch 24-hour sports-news networks and argue about 24-hour sports talk radio. And everywhere we turn, it seems, a NASCAR driver or a pro golfer or an NBA star is hawking everything from sneakers to soft drinks to Viagra.

Amid all this hoopla, it is sometimes too easy to over- look, well, the sports, the action of the athletes on the field and the court—the very essence of what speaks to us so compellingly in the first place. The fun part. For, make no mistake about it: Everywhere we turn today the finest athletes in history are performing feats of astounding virtuosity. In the old days, your grandfather might have been lucky enough to see Babe Ruth play from a distant grandstand seat. More likely, though, all he saw of the Sultan of Swat were those grainy, jerky black-and-white newsreels. Nowadays, we are techno- logically blessed. Thanks to a daily barrage of slow- motion, reverse-angle, Telestrated replays, we see it all—every home run, every slam dunk, every eagle putt, every knockout punch or photo finish. Sometimes, though, it can all start to seem commonplace. We've seen these things done so often that we have developed a kind of vicarious muscle memory. Barry Bonds launches another home run into McCovey Cove or Michelle Wei splits the fairway with a 300-yard drive, and we think "Been there, done that." But of course we really haven't.

The vast majority of us don't know what it feels like to produce such feats. And that's where this book comes in. In the following pages, you'll learn exactly what goes into 35 of the skills you see the world's best athletes performing every day. The actions assembled run the gamut from the basic to the spectacular—from the prosaic (pick up that corner-pin spare) to the death-defying (cliff-dive at Acapulco). From old school (throw the knuckleball) to too-cool-for-school (pull a motocross backflip). Through step-by-step instructions and illustrations, you'll learn the history and the essence of the skills that thrill and astound fans of every sport.

Can you try these skills at home? Well, perhaps it's better to remember that the athletes cited in these pages are men and women who have honed their bodies through countless hours of training and practice and that it might be a little late for some of us (never mind the question of innate athletic ability) to develop, say, the goal-tending fundamentals necessary even to think about stopping a breakaway; or to spend enough time in the saddle to earn a ride in the Kentucky Derby; or to get behind the wheel of a NASCAR racer. Still, learning how all these things are done should enhance your enjoyment of sports. Whether you've ever even stood on skates or not, knowing what goes into throwing—and landing—a quad will enrich your experience the next time you sit down to watch the Winter Olympics. And knowing how Michael Strahan hones in to sack the quarterback will make the next NFL game you watch that much more compelling.

You're surrounded by sports—make sure you know what's going on around you. Now, before you turn the page, be sure to warm up, stretch, and get your game face on!

MEASUREMENTS

Can't tell a 30-yard field goal from a 30-meter ski jump? Use this chart to convert the measurements in this book to the style of your choice.

1 inch = 2.54 centimeters

1 foot = 30.5 centimeters

1 yard = 0.914 meters

1 mile = 1.60 kilometers

1 pound = 0.45 kilograms

---

1 centimeter = 0.39 inches

1 meter = 1.09 yards

1 kilometer = 0.62 miles

1 kilogram = 2.20 pounds

part ONE
TEAM
sports

HOW TO STEAL HOME

Jackie Robinson did it nineteen times. "Pistol Pete" Reiser did it seven times in 1946 alone. Honus Wagner did it twice in one game, back in 1901. And Ty Cobb? Ol' Ty did it fifty-four times, including eight times in 1912.

So, with all that larceny on record, how come you have never seen a steal of home? Not the old "delayed steal," in which the runner on third, having inched his way down the line, cravenly waits until the runner on first breaks for second, drawing the throw from the catcher, and then saunters in to score. No, the real-deal steal of home is a blazing, brazen play and as rare in modern baseball as a smile from Barry Bonds.

As legendary Dodgers broadcaster Vin Scully said about Robinson, "Jackie Robinson was electrifying. Just a flame out there. Most people tell me that they're afraid of failure, and that's why they don't try to steal home. I don't think Jack had any fears at all."

Of course, Robinson also had spectacular speed. Mere guts alone won't get you the 90 feet from third base to home plate in the same time it takes the pitcher to throw the ball 60 feet, 6 inches to the exact piece of real estate you're trying to claim. You're going to need some wheels.

And you're going to need to know what you're doing. As a manager, Billy Martin was known to have the slowest player on his team pull off a steal of home plate to prove to his troops that sound fundamentals could compensate for limited physical gifts. So, in the spirit of Battlin' Billy, slip on your sliding pads and screw up your courage for that seemingly suicidal dash for glory.

1. Get on third. The ways to do this, of course, are innumerable, and not really relevant to what you are about to do. However, for sheer style points, consider that Cobb once got on first, then stole second, third, *and* home.

2. Assess the situation in the game. Ideally, there should be two outs. Any fewer and it's not worth the risk of a steal.

3. Case the pitcher. The ideal setup would feature a left-handed pitcher with a long wind-up and delivery. One reason that there are fewer steals of home in the modern era is that today's pitchers have far more

George Moriarty, who in the early years of the twentieth century played thirteen seasons in the majors, mostly for the Detroit Tigers, stole home eleven times in his career. After his playing days, Moriarty became an umpire, but he retained his larcenous heart. Tigers slugger Hank Greenberg recalls being on third in a game and having Moriarty, who was umping the base, coaching him on how to steal home. Greenberg, however, said, "I never had the guts to try."

LEGENDARY SPORTS HEROES

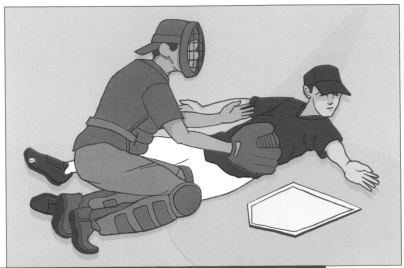

Pay dirt: A hook slide can help avoid a lunging tag.

compact deliveries than did the old-timers. You should, of course, have been studying the pitcher's delivery throughout the game, to help get your timing right for just this occasion. You should look for a breaking pitch (which will take longer to reach the plate).

4. Know your batter. Your best bet at the bat is a righty. A right-handed batter will shield the catcher's view of third and will also prevent the catcher from setting up to block the plate. Ideally, the third base-man will be playing the batter deep between second and third and will not be holding you close to the bag.

5. Work your lead. Shuffle toward the plate as the pitcher sets, being sure to keep your shoulders

squared toward the pitcher. Turning toward home
alerts the defense to your intentions. Your lead should
approach 30 feet, taking you out into what some players call "no man's land," where the pitcher will see you
peripherally.

6. Blast off. When the pitcher lifts his foot to begin
his delivery, dig in for the plate. Run low and as fast
as you can.

7. Hit the dirt. Your options are a hook slide—in which
you reach out with a leg or arm to catch the plate as
you avoid the tag from the catcher—or to simply bowl
into the catcher in an attempt to dislodge the ball and
score. Either way, you are going to raise a cloud of
dust. And, if successful, a huge roar from the crowd.

HOW TO THROW A KNUCKLEBALL

It looks goofy—faintly comical and somehow not quite worthy of the big leagues—this fluttering, floating pitch that can tie batters into undignified knots. The knuckleball is hard to swing at and even harder to catch (according to Bob Uecker, the most common tactic is to "Wait'll it stops rolling, then go pick it up").

This pitch, also known as the "floater," was first thrown by Toad Ramsey of the Louisville Colonels (later the St. Louis Browns) in the 1880s. Since then, barely 106 big leaguers have regularly thrown one. All of them understood that the key to the knuckleball is its lack of rotation.

Tim Wakefield, the Boston Red Sox's veteran righthander, has the perfect name for a knuckleballer. That's because a nonrotating ball creates a pocket, or *field,* of air in its *wake.* This wake exerts drag on the ball and,

THE EXPERTS SPEAK

When it comes to catching the knuckleball, most experts advise crossing your fingers and hoping for the best. As the legendary batting coach Charlie Lau once observed, "There are two theories on catching the knuckleball. Unfortunately, neither of the theories work."

depending on how the air swirls over the seams, creates the darting, sinking movement that makes trying to hit a knuckleball, in the words of Tim McCarver, "like trying to catch a butterfly with a pair of tweezers."

Here's how to float one of your own:

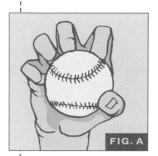

FIG. A

1. Get a grip. Curl up your fingers and wedge the ball between your thumb and your fingernails (Fig. A). The number of fingers touching the ball can vary. A knuckleballer will tell you that the best grip is the one that works for him.

2. Begin with a regular pitcher's windup. Pivot your body so you are facing third base. Raise your front leg so that your thigh is at least parallel to the ground.

3. Aim for the catcher's mask. Keep your speed in check. A perfect knuckleball can be thrown at a speed of approximately 70 mph.

4. Make the pitch. Instead of throwing the ball, simply "release" it by lifting your thumb and—at the same time—flicking with the fingers as if tossing away a piece of lint (Fig. B). Do not attempt to "push" the ball or to propel it like a shot put. Keep the wrist relatively straight.

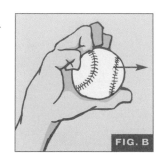

FIG. B

5. Follow through into a defensive position and be ready for anything. The only thing more unreliable than a knuckleball pitch is a knuckleball that's actually been hit.

THE EXPERTS SPEAK

Charlie Hough pitched for 25 seasons in the majors—and he owed his longevity to his mastery of the knuckleball. When asked by writer Tim Kurkjian why more pitchers didn't throw the knuckleball, Hough responded with a question of his own: "Why don't more pitchers throw 95 miles per hour? Because it's really hard to do!"

HOW TO "GUN DOWN" A RUNNER

Rifle. Cannon. Rocket. The terms used to describe an exceptional throwing arm tend to the ballistic—which is only fitting, given that an outfielder armed with such a weapon uses it like a sniper, bringing down his prey with sudden, percussive authority from a great distance. Such a play, unfolding across the entire width of the ballpark, can be one of the most electrifying moments in baseball.

Having an outfielder packing that kind of heat gives a team a significant edge. Opposing runners hesitate before trying for an extra base—or to score from third on a fly ball—often deciding that being cautious is better than being, well, mowed down. As a result, a rally can be stopped before it even begins. Andre Dawson, who played twenty-one seasons (starting in centerfield, then moving to right) for the Montreal Expos and the Chicago Cubs, had one of the most respected arms of his era. "A runner on first, with a base hit to right-center, would go first to third on every other outfielder in the league," recalls San Diego Padres superstar Tony Gwynn. "You knew not even to try it on Andre."

Gwynn, in praising Dawson's throwing, stresses his accuracy as much as his arm strength. And indeed, just as a sniper—no matter how high-powered his weapon—must perfect his aim to be effective, so must any outfielder hone his ability to hit his target with consistent accuracy. You may not have been blessed with an arm like Roberto Clemente's (in 1961 Clemente had twenty-seven outfield assists, the highest total since World War II, and a staggering number considering that, like Dawson, he was seldom challenged), but armed with the correct fundamentals you can become a respected marksman.

1. Know your target. In right field, your positioning will largely be determined by the batter at the plate. However, with a runner on third you may want to play a step or two deeper to ensure that you make any catch coming in on the ball. Keep your eye on the ball; the runner's not going anywhere until you make the catch.

2. Relax. Just as a marksman needs to squeeze, not jerk, the trigger, you want to ensure that your catch and throw are performed in an easy, fluid manner, with no herky-jerky motions. As the fly ball approaches, settle in, about a pace behind where it would land, glove up in front of you, your throwing arm slightly raised. Make the catch with your whole body going forward. Any lateral motion will put you off-balance and tend to send your throw off-line.

3. Get a grip. Grasp the ball across the seams, with the tips of your first two fingers on top of the seam. The ball should not be too deep in your hand, but rather held out toward the fingertips. An experienced player can find this grip by feel while retrieving the ball from his glove. It takes practice.

4. Form a circle. As you remove the ball from your glove and go into your throw, your arm and hand should drop down by your back hip, beginning a full circle toward the release. Your hand should not go immediately up and back, as that will rob you of fluidity and power. Your wrist should be cocked—it is very difficult to throw accurately with the wrist held rigid.

5. Let it go. With your lead shoulder pointed toward your target and your back foot perpendicular to it, step forward on your lead foot, push off from your back leg, and release the ball, allowing for a full follow-through.

Put your whole body into the throw.

6. Don't "air mail" it. While throwing a "strike" into the catcher's mitt on the fly can be very impressive, it is also risky—there's a very good chance you'll throw the ball over the catcher's head or wide down the third base line. (Such a throw also allows any other base runners to advance.) Instead, make your throw low enough that it would hit the cut-off man in the head. When he lets it through, the ball will hit the dirt and skip forward straight into the catcher's mitt, allowing him to make the tag with a minimum of wasted motion.

GREAT MOMENTS IN SPORTS HISTORY

April 11, 2001. The Oakland A's are hosting the Seattle Mariners. Bottom of the eighth, the Athletics' speedy Terrance Long on first. Ramon Hernandez singles to right. Long sees Mariners centerfielder Ichiro Suzuki, playing in just his eighth U.S. big-league game, tracking the ball into the gap, and decides to go for third. "With my speed," Long says later, "it is going to take a perfect throw to get me."

Ichiro delivers just that. Bob Finnegan of The Seattle Times called it "a 200-foot lightning bolt," and John Hickey of the Post-Intelligencer compared it to the Mona Lisa as "a thing of beauty." Everyone since has simply called it "The Throw."

HOW TO BOX OUT FOR A REBOUND

Charles Barkley retired after sixteen seasons in the NBA as one of only three players—along with Wilt Chamberlain and Kareem Abdul-Jabbar—to have at least 20,000 points, 4,000 assists, and 10,000 rebounds in a career (Karl Malone has since joined the exclusive club). Yet despite such gaudy statistics, Sir Charles is likely to be remembered as much for his outspokenness as for his accomplishments with a basketball. Ever outrageous and always enormously entertaining, Barkley made headlines and drew widespread public criticism when he said, "I am not a role model." Presumably Barkley was referring to his off-court behavior, but it seems he might just as well have been speaking of his approach to basketball fundamentals.

Coaches drilling their charges on rebounding will stress "boxing out," the technique by which a player maneuvers his or her opponent out of position under the basket in order to be able to grab the ball when it comes off the backboard. Barkley, whose prowess under the boards earned him the nickname the "Round Mound of Rebound," liked to say that he never boxed out. "I just went for the damn ball," said Sir Charles. So much for role model.

Of course, Barkley was an extraordinarily fast jumper. He got off the floor quickly, he reached his highest point quickly, and he could jump again quickly if he had to. That exceptional physical ability helped make Barkley a great rebounder. But, let's face it, just as most players can't talk with Barkley, most can't jump with him either. Other players have to box out. Even Bill Russell, whose career total of 21,620 rebounds ranks second only to Chamberlain's 23,924. Russell once told his coach on the Boston Celtics, the great Red Auerbach, "You know, Red, everything in rebounding is timing and position, because 80 percent of all rebounds are taken below the rim." And if you want position, you gotta box out.

1. Know where your man is. As the shot goes up, make sure you locate the player you are assigned to box out, even as you watch the ball in flight. One of the biggest problems with a zone defense is that it leaves a team vulnerable to surrendering offensive rebounds because each defender doesn't have a designated man to box out.

2. Get position. Slide between your opponent and the basket. Stay low, feet about shoulder width apart, arms up. Hall of Fame center Bill Walton always said that players don't keep their arms up enough on offense or defense.

3. Make contact. You'll hear coaches yelling, "Get a body on someone!" What that means is, pivot and drive your hips into your opponent. You'll also hear, "Put your butt in their gut." It doesn't get any clearer than that. Plant your rear in your opponent's midsection.

Read the shot

Stay between opponent and basket

Plant rear In opponent's midsection

Everything in rebounding is timing and position.

This will allow you to feel which way he or she is sliding and to hold him or her back, giving yourself a buffer zone in which to aim for the rebound. If you don't have direct contact, your opponent can get around you.

Dennis Rodman, a player who believed in both boxing out and thinking out of the box, holds the NBA record for most consecutive seasons leading the league in rebounds. The flamboyant Rodman had the NBA's most boards from 1991–92 through 1997–98.

4. Read the shot. As the shot goes up, keep your eyes on the ball but continue driving against your opponent, gauging his motions. You should be able to determine which way the ball is going to come off the backboard: A ball shot from the right corner will bounce toward the left corner a high percentage of the time.

5. Explode upward. Coming off the contact with your opponent, almost like a bumper car, jump for the ball. This is where a little of Sir Charles's just going for "the damn ball" comes in.

6. Get big. As you go up for the carom, spread out your body. Take up room, keeping your opponent away from the ball. Don't worry too much about making contact. It almost never happens that a player in front will be called for a foul. The refs always get the player who's behind if he or she has been boxed out properly. Kevin McHale, who pulled down his share of rebounds during his Hall of Fame career with the Celtics, used to say that you could even get away with a little shove as the ball went up, because everyone's eyes, including the refs', will be on the arc of the ball.

Sometimes you have to go back to school to remember the fundamentals. That's what happened to Knicks guard Penny Hardaway when he visited a youth summer basketball camp in August 2004. As the NBA star sat surrounded by admiring fans, Coach Al Brathway drilled the kids on the importance of boxing out. The exchange went something like this:

Coach: "Do you have aspirations to play high school basketball?"

Children: "Yes!"

Coach: "Then you've got to box out! Do you have aspirations to play college basketball?"

Children: "Yes!"

Coach: "Then you've got to box out! Do you have aspirations to play in the NBA?"

Children: "Yes!"

Brathway: "Then don't worry about it—there, nobody boxes out!"

Hardaway took the joke in stride, and the kids cheered.

RULES OF THE GAME

BASKETBALL

HOW TO DUNK

Slam. Jam. Throw down. Stuff. In your face. Phi Slamma Jamma. Throw it down, big man!

No move in sports carries as much attitude as the slam dunk. The dunk is all about 'tude. You get the same two points for a layup that you do for a dunk, and coaches the world over would probably rather see their charges take the safe, if stodgy, approach of kissing it off the glass rather than risk missing or, worse, injuring themselves throwing down a rim-rattling dunk. But if you're interested in making not just a basket, but a statement—and if you've got the ups to play not just above the rim, but above your opponents, why would you ever pass up the chance to fly?

The dunk has been around for as long as really tall men have been putting basketballs through hoops, but the slam really took off—and became an iconic part of the game—back in the 1970s, in the heyday of the old ABA (American Basketball Association). The godfather of the dunk, of course, was Julius Erving—Dr. J. In his first pro game with the Virginia Colonels, the 6'7" Erving dunked over the Kentucky Colonels' 7'2" Artis Gilmore and 6'9" Dan Issel. He never looked back—or down. Erving's high-flying dunks defined his league and changed the face of basketball. One of the seminal moments in the sport remains the 1976 ABA All-Star Game, at which, during halftime, the first slam dunk contest was staged. Erving's astounding dunk, which featured a take-off from the free-throw line, won the contest and, thanks to a million Dr. J posters featuring him in full flight, became the inspiration for the generation that followed.

Here's how to do it yourself. And before you say you're not big enough to jam it, recall that the 1986 NBA Slam Dunk Contest was won by Spud Webb—all 5'7" of him.

1. Get a grip. If your hand is big enough, you will be able to palm the ball, which makes bringing it up above the rim much easier. If you can't consistently palm the basketball, you should perform a two-handed dunk.

2. Get up to speed. Dribble toward the basket at a fast, aggressive pace. Use the same approach pattern as you would for a layup. (For a righthander, that means starting from the far right end of the free throw line, dribbling toward the basket with your right hand, eyes focused on the square just above the rim.)

3. Pick it up. Gather up the ball from your dribble about 12 feet in front of the basket. Continue fast toward the basket, taking the two steps allowed by the rules as you either settle the ball into your palm or else grip it firmly in both hands.

> **FOR THE RECORD**
>
> *On April 1, 2000, the Harlem Globetrotters' Mike "Wild Thing" Wilson successfully dunked on a 12-foot basket in Conseco Fieldhouse in Indianapolis, setting a record for the highest slam.*

If you can't palm the ball, go for the two-hand slam.

4. Take off. Jump from your second step, and drive forcefully, with as much explosive power as you can muster, up toward the rim.

5. Stretch it. Extend your arm—or arms, if you're doing a two-handed dunk—toward the basket, aiming just above the rim.

6. Slam it! Jam the ball down through the rim. Do not hang on the rim unless you have to in order to avoid landing on another player. Some players like to hang on the rim because it looks cool (and reminds every-body, "Hey, I was all the way up here"), but it is a very dangerous move. Not only do you run the risk of bringing down the backboard in a Darryl Dawkins–like shower of glass, but there's also a good chance of getting submarined by another player and coming down on top of him or, worse, upside down.

> **THE EXPERTS SPEAK**
>
> *"I hope that 10 years from now this isn't a big deal. That would be my dream: That 10 years from now three or four girls enter the dunk contest and it's not a big deal."*—Candace Parker, after beating five male competitors to win the 2004 POWERade Jam Fest. Parker, a 6´3˝ 17-year-old from Naperville, Ill., earned a near-perfect score of 79 (out of 80) for her eyes-covered final slam.

7. Land it. Come down on both feet—and avoid the urge to trash talk the poor guy (or girl) you just dunked over.

BASKETBALL

HOW TO BLOCK A SHOT

As a budding hoops star at Notre Dame, Amanda Barksdale had a lofty ambition: The 6´3˝ center from Friendswood, Texas, told the school's paper that what she really wanted was to block a shot in spectacular fashion. "One of my goals," she said, "is to send one into the crowd, all the way up to the blue seats."

Certainly there is no more dramatic a defensive play in basketball than the emphatically blocked shot. A real "No-soup-for-you!" rejection can not only prevent a basket, it can also demoralize an opponent and fire up the crowd. But as thrilling and soul-satisfying as a block that rockets the ball all the way to the refreshment stands might be, such a play is usually not as desirable as a more contained and considered block. Bill Russell, perhaps the premier defensive center in NBA history, was a master at blocking shots but keeping the ball in play, so that his Celtics teammates could get the defensive rebound and run the fast break. "It wasn't a good defensive play until

RULES OF THE GAME

Goaltending is called if the defender interferes with the ball on the rim or after it has begun its downward path toward the basket. The shooting team receives two points (or three, if the goaltending occurred on a three-point attempt).

you had possession of the ball going the other way," Russell often said. As Red Auerbach, Russell's coach on those great Boston teams, wrote in his autobiography, "You never saw Russell bat a ball into the third balcony." Instead, Auerbach explained, Russell concentrated on where the ball went after the block: "He would block the shot by reaching underneath the ball, or on the side if he had to. He would pop the ball straight up and grab it like a rebound, or else redirect it into the hands of one of his teammates." Russell's blocks, in effect, became four-point plays: the two points his opponents didn't get and the two points the Celtics did.

Here's how you can start putting points on the board:

1. Play off your man. Help out defensively by coming across the lane to contest shots. This frees up your teammates to play looser and more aggressively on the perimeter. It also allows you to initiate your block while on the move, rather than from a standstill.

2. Know your opponent. While much of shot-blocking success depends on an innate ability or instinct to recognize when the player you are facing is going to shoot, a careful study—either on film, or simply by watching closely during the game—of his or her

> *The record for the most blocked shots in an NBA game was set by the Los Angeles Lakers' seven-foot center Elmore Smith, who on Oct. 28, 1973 rejected seventeen shots by the Portland Trail Blazers.*

FOR THE RECORD

stance and habits will help you recognize when a shot is going up. In any event, keep your eyes on your opponent's torso, to avoid being thrown by any head or shoulder fakes.

3. Think early. It is better to jump too early than to go up too late and risk a goaltending call. An early jump that doesn't result in an official blocked shot may still alter the shooter's approach enough to prevent a basket—call it a block that doesn't appear in the box score.

4. Go straight up. Keep your arms straight above you and don't flail in an attempt to swat the ball away. This will help keep your body away from your opponent and avoid drawing a whistle.

5. Raise a hand. If possible, use the hand opposite the one the shooter is using. If he's shooting right-handed, extend your left straight up. If she's shooting from the left, raise your right. This gives you an extra four to six inches in height, as you aren't reaching across your body. It will also help you avoid getting your arm tangled with your opponent's and getting called for a foul.

> **RULES OF THE GAME**
>
> *A defensive player is credited with a blocked shot when he or she alters the course of a shot—preventing it from going through the hoop—by making contact with the ball after it has left the shooter's hands.*

Soup's off! Jump early to get
the ball on the way up.

6. **Know where your teammates are.** Like Russell,
try to hit the ball from the side, or even pop it from
underneath, to direct it toward a teammate for a
defensive rebound.

HOW TO CATCH A PASS OVER THE MIDDLE

"For who? For what?" Those immortal words, uttered by Philadelphia Eagles running back Ricky Watters in 1995, will stand forever as testimony to how a football player must never think. Watters' quote is, in fact, perversely inspiring, a brazenly bad-example counterpoint to British climber George Mallory's stirring "Because it's there" explanation for why he sought to conquer Mount Everest. Watters reached his pinnacle of cravenness in a postgame press conference after the Eagles lost their '95 season opener to the Tampa Bay Buccaneers 21-6. The reporters asked why he had, in the closing stages of the game, bailed out on trying to catch a pass over the middle, obviously short-arming his attempt in order to avoid being hit by the defenders. Watters—who had arrived in Philadelphia that season as a multimillion-dollar free agent from the San Francisco 49ers—drew himself up to his full 6′1″, 211 pounds and indignantly replied, "I'm not going to trip up there and get knocked out. For who? For what?"

As the old saying goes, "If you have to ask, you'll never know." And you'll never make the catch. Football players take punishment. That's what they do—in practice, in scrimmages, and on every play of every game. Collision and concussion are the daily coin of the gridiron. But some moments carry extra peril and promise extra pain.

Foremost of these is a receiver's going up for a pass while running a route that takes him across the field.

A receiver running a pass route that takes him to the outside of the field, that is, toward the sideline, usually has only two defenders to contend with: the cornerback and the safety. But a receiver who cuts the other way, inside, across the middle, will draw the attention of the cornerback and the safety, plus two or three linebackers and perhaps even the other safety. That's a lot of defensive firepower targeting one man. A receiver running a route across the middle needs speed, athleticism, focus—and a whole lot more motivation than Ricky Watters brought to the task.

1. Know what you're facing. The crossing pattern works well against man-to-man coverage (in which each defensive back and linebacker covers an individual receiver), especially when two receivers cross over the middle.

2. Watch the snap. If you're playing as a flanker back, you'll be lined up outside of the tight end—say to the right side—and a step back from the line of scrimmage. Receivers line up in either a three-point "sprinter's stance" (bent over, legs split and knees bent, with one foot slightly in front of the other, the opposite hand on the ground), or else an erect stance (standing straight up, one foot slightly in front of the other, hands at your sides). In either case, your head should be turned toward the center, to make sure you see the snap. Like the old saying goes, keep your eye on the ball.

3. Fight for your route. When the ball is snapped, bring both arms and hands up to ward off a hit from the defensive back. (Defensive players are allowed to make contact with receivers—"bump and run"—only in the first five yards off the line of scrimmage.) Duck

Don't let approaching "footsteps" distract you from the ball.

your shoulder under the D-back's hands, and lunge upward and away from his grasp. This technique is known as the "dip-and-rip." An alternative technique is the "swim," in which you use your hands to slap the defender's arms to the side while you move in the opposite direction, then swing your outside arm up and over the defender like a swimmer doing the crawl, propelling him behind you.

4. Focus on your route. Part of the defensive back's intent in making contact off the line is to disrupt your concentration and throw you off your pattern. You should be clear now. Run straight down field for ten yards, then cut toward the inside of the field.

5. Look for the hole. Run your pattern, but be aware of where the defenders are. Don't look for the ball too soon.

6. Sight the ball. Once the ball is thrown, keep your focus on it. A glance around for a defender can cause you to miss the catch. Your hands and arms should be extended from your body. Don't let the ball bounce off your shoulder or chest.

7. Secure the football. Tuck the ball away immediately into your armpit. Don't try to run before you have the ball.

8. Prepare to be hit. Look at it this way: You're going to get nailed whether you make the catch or not. So you might as well make it.

Jerry Rice, just about everybody's pick as the greatest receiver in NFL history, took his share of hits during his Hall of Fame career. A few catches over the middle left him with concussions, but the hardest bell-ringing Rice ever took was against the Buffalo Bills in 1992. Rice made the catch, but was driven into the turf by Bills defender Phil Hansen. When the trainers reached the unconscious Rice, he was snoring on the field. Doctors had to wake him up to diagnose another concussion.

Maybe all those hits were part of what made Rice such an aggressive and effective blocking receiver. "Throwing a block— that's your only time to get back at the defensive backs."

HOW TO SACK THE QUARTERBACK

"We're like a bunch of animals, kicking and clawing and scratching at each other."

That was David "Deacon" Jones's description of the struggles that go on between the offensive linemen protecting the quarterback and the defensive players attempting to get to that quarterback and drive him into the turf. And the Deacon should know. Jones, who played fourteen seasons in the NFL as a defensive end, probably planted more quarterbacks than any other player in the history of the game.

Fittingly enough, it was Jones who coined the term "sack," a wonderfully descriptive term for the tackling of a quarterback behind the line of scrimmage. It was an old hunting term, for when you've bagged your quarry. Picture a shotgunned duck dropped into a burlap sack. Unfortunately, the NFL didn't start keeping official stats on sacks until 1982—eight years after Jones retired. Had anyone been keeping official track, Jones would likely still be the all-time leader in the category he named and defined. (As it is, the record is held by Reggie White, who, during his fifteen-year career with the Philadelphia Eagles and the Green Bay Packers, amassed 198 sacks.)

The thing about Deacon's description of the combat that went on over the pass rush is that, while it captures the violence and the intensity of the action, it shortchanges the cerebral side. For pass rushers, despite their 300-plus pounds of hurtling ferocity and dogged determination, must also be supreme tacticians—as prepared and focused as generals going into battle. So focused, in fact, that, as Michael Strahan—the New York Giants defensive end who in 2001 set the season record for sacks with twenty-two and a half—described it to *Sports Illustrated*, "Half the time when you get [a sack] you don't know you got it. You don't hear anything. . . . You filter it."

Only when the play is over, said Strahan, does the filter come off. "The crowd lets you know how big a play it is. It can turn the game."

In today's NFL, being a pass rusher is a glamour job, filled by men who possess a rare combination of size, speed, athleticism, and smarts. They are paid accordingly, and they work hard at their craft, studying hundreds of hours of video (in addition to their work on the field) in an effort to find the one tiny key that will give them the slightest jump toward that quarterback. For make no mistake: As the Deacon preached, the whole point is to drive that guy into the ground.

1. Know your situation. You're the defensive end, lined up on the left side. Take stock of the game: Down, field position, score, time remaining—all these factors will help you determine whether the play is likely to be a pass, and whether you will have a shot at the quarterback.

2. Read the offense. Where is the running back? Is he going to try to block you? Is the tackle straining forward, or is he leaning back, setting up to block you for a pass? If the receiver is in motion, watch his steps; some will slow slightly in anticipation of turning into his pass pattern, which will happen just as the ball is snapped. Watch the center. Most will give some clue—a squeeze of the ball, a flex of the calf—when they are about to make the snap. All of these details should be familiar to you from pre-game scouting and study.

3. Cash in on your setup. Your chance of a successful pass rush on any play is largely determined by how you've played throughout the game. You "set up" the opposing tackle, say, by repeatedly showing him the same moves, run at the same intensity, on early downs. Lull him into expecting a certain rush, and then change it up for the big play.

4. Plan your moves. Have a definite idea of how you're going to get past your man. Are you going to "rip and dip" (knock his arm away with yours and then sharply drop your shoulder to go around him)? Are you going to "swim," windmilling your arms around the offensive lineman's to push him down and behind you? Are you going to try to run around him, replacing a game-long pattern of power collisions with a sudden burst of speed? Make a choice and stick with it.

5. Think forward. Your first step should always be toward the quarterback. Even if you're trying to run around your man, you'll want to "shorten the corner."

6. Don't waste time. Keep the juking and shaking to a minimum. You have less than two seconds before the quarterback releases the ball. Don't spend it dancing.

7. Don't quit. Even after you turn the corner on your man, he may grab or hold or try to tackle you. Just

It takes smarts and "animal instinct" to make the sack.

keep going. Drag him to the quarterback, if you have to. Remember Deacon Jones's "bunch of animals."

8. Finish. Hit the quarterback with everything you have, wrapping up him and the ball. But just remember: no taunting and absolutely no sack dances.

Mark Gastineau, the New York Jets defensive end whose twenty-two sacks in 1984 stood as the NFL record until Michael Strahan broke it with twenty-two and a half in 2001, became a professional boxer after retiring from football. Though he won his first nine fights by knockout, as a boxer Gastineau was a terrific football player. He was beaten in his tenth bout by journeyman Tim Anderson and eventually retired with a record of 15-2.

LEGENDARY SPORTS HEROES

HOW TO BLOCK A PUNT

In the first quarter of a September 2000 game between the Tampa Bay Buccaneers and the Detroit Lions in Pontiac, Michigan, Bucs defensive back Ronde Barber was jogging off the field as the teams were lining up in preparation for a Detroit punt. Just then Tampa Bay special teams coach Joe Marciano made an adjustment in coverage and sent Barber back onto the field. Upon the snap, Barber charged through and knocked down the punt by the Lions' John Jett. Marciano, it appeared, had masterfully orchestrated a game-breaking play. Barber, however, suggested that it might not have been quite so impressively preplanned. "Joe said, 'Go block the punt,' so I went out and blocked the punt," explained Barber after the Bucs' 31-10 victory. "It's an easy game sometimes."

It's an easy game, all right—if you know what you're doing.

A punting team faces a trade-off between protecting the kicker and getting men down the field to cover the receiver. In a "tight punt" formation, the kicker is about ten yards behind the center, and the other nine players are grouped closely around. In a "spread punt" formation, which is the scheme used by most NFL teams today, two cover men, on opposite ends of the line, are sent down the field as soon as the ball is snapped. To prevent the punt being blocked, the kicker will be farther back, 13 to 15 yards behind the center.

The defensive team can decide to make an all-out effort to block a punt. To do so, they will send both linebackers— who normally stay back, watching the play develop and guarding against a fake punt—up to the line, leaving only the defensive halfbacks in position to defend against a run or pass. The safety will play deep downfield to receive the punt.

Regardless of whether the linebackers charge or not, the players with the best shot at blocking the punt are the defensive ends. Though they have to come from farther outside, they can penetrate very quickly. So, if you're a defensive end and your coach tells you to block a punt, just think like Ronde Barber.

1. Know your time frame. If the opposing center is slow delivering the ball, you have a shot; if the kicker takes more than two steps, he may be vulnerable. Time is of the essence: Most coaches use 2.1 seconds as the cutoff. Against a team that can consistently get the ball off in less than that time, blocking a punt is going to be difficult. A team slower than that, however, should be considered vulnerable.

2. Know your target. Remember that the kicker will be striding into the ball as he punts, coming forward a little more than four yards from the point at which he takes the snap. Rushing at the kicker will very likely carry you too deep, past the ball and into the punter, drawing a penalty for roughing the kicker.

3. Blast off. At the snap, the defensive tackle next to you will attempt to charge through the gap between the offensive guard and the tackle, to engage the "upback," who is playing behind the center. While he keeps his men occupied, you should shoot past the offensive tackle—slapping him aside if you have to—toward the punter. It generally takes .6 seconds for the snap to reach the center. You have to be well on your way.

Launch yourself at a spot in front of the punter.

4. Make yourself big. Come in with both arms raised and hands together. Aim for a spot four-and-a-half yards in front of where the punter received the snap and you should be like an interceptor missile. Don't launch yourself through the air, however, as you run the risk of colliding with the punter.

5. Follow the ball. If you do get a hand on the ball and knock it down, be prepared to retrieve it and run, or to block for a teammate who picks it up.

Coach Marciano was a little more explicit in his instructions to Ronde Barber when Tampa Bay faced the Bengals in 2001. Having noticed that the Bengals' punter was vulnerable to a blitz from the corner, Marciano went to Barber a few days before the game and asked his cornerback, "Do you want to block a punt this week?" Barber said he did, and, sure enough, on the Bengals' first punt of the game, Barber came in on a lightning blitz and batted down the punt. Tampa Bay tight end Todd Yoder picked up the loose ball and ran it 11 yards for a touchdown, putting the Bucs ahead.

GREAT MOMENTS
IN SPORTS
HISTORY

HOW TO DEFEND AGAINST A BREAKAWAY

Every team sport has its moments of one-on-one confrontation—pitcher staring down batter in baseball, defensive back and receiver going up for the pass in football, two centers banging under the boards in basketball. But for sheer mano a mano drama nothing matches a breakaway in hockey. It's a Dodge City gunfight on ice. And it can change the momentum of a game in the flick of a wrist.

A breakaway occurs when the player with the puck gets past the opposing team's defensemen, leaving only the goalie between him (or her) and the net. Should the attacking player be illegally checked or impeded at this point, game play stops. The puck is placed at center ice, and the player receives a free try at a goal, with no defenders other than the goalie on the ice. On a normal penalty, the attacking player gets only one shot. On a breakaway, however, the goalie must contend not only with the initial shot, but also with any rebounds, as well as with the arrival of other opposing players.

Vladislav Tretiak, the legendary goalie of the great Soviet national squads, once said, "There is no position in sport as noble as that of goal tending," and it is precisely that fierce pride and sense of self that a goalie must call upon to defend successfully against the breakaway. Hockey

people say that average goalies react, good goalies anticipate, and great goalies influence. That is, when defending
the net against an oncoming skater, you should always be
attempting to dictate the action, to position yourself and
move in such a way that the attacker ends up taking the
shot you want him or her to take.

1. Know your enemy. Assess the player coming at
you as soon as he crosses the blue line. What are his
tendencies? What are his strengths and weaknesses?
Most important, is the player a shooter or a deker? A
shooter will go right for the shot; a deker will first try
to get you out of position—and then shoot.

**2. Focus on the puck (not on the player's eyes or
body).** Look where he carries the puck on his stick. If
he's holding it to the side, there is a chance he could
be readying to shoot. If he is carrying it directly out in
front, expect a deke, as it is difficult to shoot from that
position.

3. Take your challenge position. Assume a confident, decidedly noble position two to three feet in
front of the crease. Don't go out too far.

4. Back it up. Begin skating backward after the
attacker has entered the slot between the circles,
about 20 to 25 feet in front of the net. Make sure of your
speed: too fast and you'll give the shooter too much
net; too slow and he'll get around you. Mike Richter,
who had four shutouts during the 1994 NHL playoffs

Know which holes you cover best—and make the shooter aim there.

while leading the New York Rangers to the Stanley
Cup, and who stopped twelve of the thirteen penalty
shots he faced in his career, was particularly effective
because of his ability to back up at the same speed as
the shooter was coming in.

5. Show him an opening. Play to your strengths. If
you're confident in your glove hand, for instance, show
him the 2-hole, encouraging him to beat you there (see
diagram). Vary this, however, to avoid being predictable.

6. Anticipate the rebound. Once you've forced his hand, and maximized your chances of making the save, be sure you are in position to control the puck after the shot. You want this play to end quietly.

Looking for confidence against the breakaway? Look no further than Dominik Hasek. Once, during a breakaway drill in practice, the Red Wings' great net minder stopped thirty-one straight shots.

GREAT MOMENTS IN SPORTS HISTORY

HOCKEY

HOW TO SHOOT A SLAP SHOT

Drafted by the Calgary Flames in 1981, Al MacInnis became an NHL regular when he was called up for good on December 14, 1983. The 20-year-old from Inverness, Nova Scotia, wasted little time in establishing his bona fides: In a game against the Blues in St. Louis on January 17, 1984, MacInnis broke goalie Mike Liut's mask with a slap shot launched from outside the blue line. Over the next twenty seasons, MacInnis would establish himself as one of the finest defensemen in the history of the league—with a slap shot second to none. Just five months before he turned 40, MacInnis won his seventh NHL Hardest Shot competition at the 2003 All-Star Game, rocketing a slap shot into the net at 99 mph. And, unlike the majority of modern NHLers, whose sticks are made of space-age carbon and graphite composites, MacInnis was wielding old-fashioned wood— which, frighteningly enough, actually took a few miles per hour *off* his shot.

For extra surprise and effectiveness, take your slap shots hot off a pass. Like a basketball dunk off an "alley-oop," this move—known as "one-timing"—gives the goalie no time to react.

RULES OF THE GAME

"That guy's a freak," said Philadelphia's Jeremy Roenick

of the player who earned the nickname "Chopper." "I'm never getting in front of one of his shots. I'll tell you that."

A wise decision, considering that in his career MacInnis broke the arms of at least two goalies—the Chicago Black Hawks' Jocelyn Thibault and Chris Osgood of the Detroit Red Wings—with his slap shot. Of course, MacInnis wasn't just dangerous with that slashing slap—he was also superbly effective. Seven times he scored 20 or more goals in a season, and his total of 1,274 points through 2004 was the highest among active defensemen.

The slap shot is hockey's equivalent of the slam dunk or the knockout punch (well, along with the actual knockout punch occasionally thrown during a brawl), a spectacular, pyrotechnic display of power that can bring a crowd to their feet in an instant. The rap on the slap is that it is inaccurate and easy for a defenseman to block. Still, when executed properly and from the right spot, the shot can be very effective. And, while a slap shot the caliber of MacInnis's is indeed freakish, most players can develop a fairly authoritative delivery that can give a goalie fits.

1. Get to the point. In hockey, "the point" is the location of a defenseman anywhere along the attacking blue line. This spot, at least 60 feet from the goal, is one of the best locations from which to try a slap shot.

2. Take a stand. Or stance. Your feet should be a little wider than shoulder width apart, and your body should be turned almost perpendicular to the net, so that your

A stick's flex gives bone-snapping pop to the slap shot.

upper shoulder (the left, for a right-handed shooter) is pointed toward the goal. The puck should be centered between your feet, and out in front of you enough so that it is visible when you look straight down.

3. Drop your hand. While keeping your top hand in its normal spot at the top of your stick, slide your bottom hand six to eight inches down the handle toward the blade. This will give you more weight in your shot.

4. Windup. Don't take a huge backswing, as that will telegraph your shot and give the goalie more time to react. Bring your stick back to just above waist height.

5. Shift the weight. As you swing the stick, transfer your weight from your back skate onto your front, striding into the shot as you swing through your shoulders.

6. Keep your eye on the puck. On other shots, players never look at the puck, but with such a long windup, it's essential that you keep focused on the target, just as you would hitting a baseball or a golf ball.

7. Hit the ice. Your stick should actually hit the ice first, just behind the puck—and just as you complete your weight transfer. Keep a strong grip with your bottom hand. The shaft of your stick will bend slightly and then snap back to hit the puck, propelling it forward with maximum power.

Slap shots can do a lot of damage—and not only on the scoreboard. Just ask Bob Baun. In Game Six of the 1964 Stanley Cup finals, the Toronto Maple Leafs defenseman took a Gordie Howe slap shot off his right foot. Baun knew instantly that a bone was broken. Carried off the ice on a stretcher, he had the Leafs' trainer give him a shot of painkiller and tape up his ankle. Then Baun went back out on the ice. Two minutes into overtime he scored the winning goal. Two nights later, Baun played a regular shift in Game Seven, as Toronto won and clinched the Stanley Cup. "The best break I ever had," says Baun of Howe's zinger.

LEGENDARY SPORTS HEROES

SOCCER

HOW TO SCORE A PENALTY KICK

No pressure. No pressure at all. It was only the final game of the 1999 Women's World Cup, U.S. versus China, with a crowd of 90,185 people (including President Bill Clinton) at the Rose Bowl—the largest crowd ever for a women's-only sporting event. Brandi Chastain was about to take the fifth penalty kick for the United States. With the score tied 0-0 after regulation and two 15-minute overtime periods, the game had gone to a shootout and, thanks to a diving save by U.S. keeper Briana Scurry on China's fifth shot, the tally was 4-4. With a successful kick, Chastain would win the game. And the tournament.

> *The penalty kick was introduced into the game of soccer in 1891. The first major World* **FOR THE RECORD** *Cup game to be decided on penalty kicks was West Germany's 1982 semifinals victory over France.*

"Like a showdown at high noon," was how Chastain, in an interview with *ABC Sports*, described the situation as she faced off against the Chinese goalkeeper. "The only thing that was going through my mind was 'Don't look at her.'"

The penalty kick, in which a player is given a free shot from a spot 12 yards directly in front of the net, occurs during regulation time when a team has committed a major foul within its own penalty area. It can also be part of a shootout, which is used to settle any game still tied after two overtimes. In the free-flowing world of soccer, it is a rare moment of set, one-on-one confrontation. And, as such, it is a moment of supreme psychological drama. The kicker, of course, has a tremendous advantage: The goalie has about two-tenths of a second to stop a shot, coming at 70 mph, from entering a 24-foot-by-8-foot net. It is virtually impossible to stop a well-struck, well-aimed shot from going in. Yet, statistically, more than 20 percent of penalty kicks fail. Italy lost the 1994 World Cup final when the great Roberto Baggio failed to convert his penalty kick during the shootout. Pelé himself preferred not to take penalty kicks. The intense pressure of the situation can make even the most fearsome strikers tighten up.

For her part, Chastain kept her cool in the heat of Pasadena. "Just like it was practice," was how she would later describe the curving left-footer she deposited in the right side of the net to give the U.S. the title. That's when Chastain—presumably not just like it was practice—ripped off her jersey and, clad in the world's most famous black sports bra, dropped to her knees on the turf in celebration. Emotions run high on penalty kicks.

1. Remember to breathe. You'll be alone out there on the pitch, your teammates 20 yards away beyond the penalty arc, and every eye in the stadium will be on you. And did we mention that you are expected to make the shot? Seriously, take a blow.

2. Know your own strength. If you prefer to blast the ball, you'll want to strike it with the laces of your shoe. This technique will put maximum power and pace on your shot, but you'll be giving up some control. If, on the other hand, you're looking for the most possible accuracy, prepare to use a "push" shot, striking the ball with the inside of your foot while opening your hips. You could also choose to play a "cut" shot, striking the ball with the instep. This technique gives you the best blend of power and accuracy.

3. Make up your mind. Decide where you intend to place your shot, and don't waver during your approach—no matter what the goalie does. The shooter's second-guessing herself is perhaps the leading cause of failed penalty kicks. The most promising targets are the high and low corners on each side of the net (see diagram).

Sure shots: Aim for a high or low corner on either side of the net.

4. Keep your eyes on the ball and your target—not on the goalie. New rules allow the goalie to move laterally along the goal line (but not forward) before the shot. And every keeper will try to distract the shooter with upper body movement.

5. Don't tip your hand (or, rather, your foot). A savvy goalie will be able to tell where the shot is headed from the angle at which a kicker approaches the ball, or by how she turns her foot.

6. Hound the rebound. On a penalty kick during a game, if the keeper stops the kick but can't keep hold of the ball, the kicker or any member of his team can score on the rebound. If your shot hits the post or crossbar, however, you can't score until one of your teammates touches the ball.

If you do score, that's when it's time to whip off the jersey—sports bra or not.

HOW TO PERFORM A BICYCLE KICK

The following sentence appears in a report detailing a 2002 study conducted by the University of Sao Paulo's Biophysics Laboratory: "Any movement in nature must obey Newton's laws of motion, but football adds something on top of that; in its essence, football is a combination of force and speed as well as skill and creativity—a supreme blend of rationality and irrationality."

By "football", of course, the scientists were referring to the game Americans call soccer. The subject of their study? "The Biomechanics of Pelé's Bicycle Kick." Certainly there are phenomena far less worthy of scientific examination. And as for blending skill and creativity (with a heavy dose of irrationality), the act of flinging oneself into midair to kick a ball backward over one's head would sure seem to fit the bill. It is, to put it mildly, something you don't see every day.

Indeed, the bicycle kick, which by its nature tends to be used in the game's most dramatic or desperate moments— on set scoring opportunities or when a ball is headed toward the net and must be cleared—is as spectacular and memorable a move as any in sport. Ramon Unzaga of Spain is generally credited with being the first player to use the bicycle kick, in 1914. Unzaga later immigrated to Chile, and so impressed were the South American sportswriters with the kick that they dubbed it the *chilena.* In the 1930s and '40s, Leonidas da Silva, Brazil's first professional soccer superstar, perfected the bicycle kick. It became, of course, the signature move of another Brazilian player of note— and subject of scientific inquiry—the great Pelé. In later years Hugo Sanchez of Mexico and Argentine superstar Diego Maradona would also put their own stamps on the move.

Before attempting the bicycle kick, remember that the move is a dangerous one. By falling incorrectly, you can injure your hands, wrists, back, or head. Consider, also, that the move is a one-shot gamble. It is easy to miss and land on the turf looking foolish. Succeed, though—especially if your shot goes into the net—and you are a hero. Just ask Pelé.

1. Choose your opportunity. The bicycle kick is largely a reaction shot, to be attempted when your positioning and the height and direction of the ball do not allow for a more conventional kick or header.

2. Relax. Despite its pyrotechnic image, the bicycle kick does not require a full-power blast. The sweep of your leg and body will propel the ball.

3. Maintain your visual. With your back to your target, keep your eye on the ball—which may be coming from behind or from either side—tracking it until it connects with your foot.

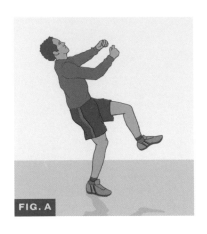

FIG. A

FIG. B

FIG. C

FIG. D

4. Jump off of one leg. You should drive off of your kicking leg while flinging your other leg, bent at about a 45-degree angle, straight up to initiate lift (Fig. A).

5. Rock-scissor. As you rise, rock your body backward (Fig. B). Just as you reach your peak and begin to drop back, snap your kicking leg—bent at the knee—toward the ball, while at the same time bringing your other leg down. Your legs will scissor, providing the pop for your kick.

6. Level off. Your back should be parallel to the ground at the moment your foot makes contact with the ball (Fig. C). This will impart the ideal angle on your kick.

7. Touch down. As you fall back to the pitch, spread your arms and hands to absorb the impact (Fig. D) and twist your body to the opposite side from your kicking foot to avoid landing flat.

Be sure to have your goal-scoring reaction dance ready.

Marcelo Balboa's soaring, scoring bicycle kick for the Colorado Rapids against the Columbus Crew was named Major League Soccer's Goal of the Year for 2000 by one Internet poll. He learned the move as a child by practicing on his parents' bed—"when they were not home"—with a Nerf ball.

TRAINING TIP

part TWO
SOLO
sports

AUTO RACING

HOW TO MAKE IT THROUGH "THE BIG ONE"

Sometime in 2004, the NASCAR Dad officially ran the Soccer Mom and her minivan off the road. There are some 75 million NASCAR fans in the United States, with more catching the high-octane bug every day. An average of more than 100,000 pack the stands at each race, with 20 million more tuning in on TV. These fans, from Florida to New Hampshire to California, thrill to the speed, the color, the sheer shake-your-soul noise—and, yes, the danger—of this fastest of all American sports. For the 43 men who get behind the wheel to compete each week, the stakes are far higher than just a winner's check and a kiss from Miss Budweiser. If you're off by an inch in this sport, you're not just talking bogey instead of par, or an extra man on base.

You're talking a very ugly smudge on the wall. So when you take to the track, you had better be very sure of your skills.

Technology plays a huge role in NASCAR, and teams devote thousands of hours and millions of dollars to squeezing the last mph out of their race cars,

"I guess one good thing about it is everybody is going the same speed, so when they hit, they really don't hit that hard."

THE EXPERTS SPEAK

— Bobby Labonte, commenting after a 24-car pile-up at Talladega in 2002 but in the end it's the guy in the driver's seat who makes the difference—and whose butt, quite literally, is on the line. The green flag falls, the crowd roars, and the crew chief hollers over the in-car radio, "Drive it like you stole it, son," and for the next three hours you can't let down for a split second.

As driver Wally Dallenbach put it to *USA Today*, racing in NASCAR is "like being in a train wreck for three hours. The concentration level is just unbelievable." NASCAR racing is always a close, nose-to-tail, fender-to-fender, paint-trading affair, and when one car gets into trouble, spinning or hitting the wall, others can easily get caught up in the mayhem. On the high bankings of the superspeedways, however, where the cars are required to run with restrictor plates on their carburetors to keep speeds down ("down" being a relative term: these guys are still going 190-plus), huge packs develop with cars running three and four wide, drafting each other and separated by mere inches. When something goes wrong here, it can touch off a devastating multicar melee with a dozen or more racers spinning, ricocheting off the walls, and colliding in a cloud of tire smoke thick enough to obscure half the track. Drivers call such incidents "the Big One"—and the question on the superspeedways is not if the Big One will happen, but when.

When it does, to make it through, you're going to need skill, help from above, and a bit of luck.

1. Be cool. NASCAR drivers have honed their skills through years of racing and testing. With so many miles behind the wheel, they develop an extraordinary feel for their cars and an instinctive sense of the action around them on the racetrack, as well as for the unfolding course of the race. The best way to avoid trouble—besides jumping out to an early lead—is to avoid pressing too hard. You should be driving relaxed and within the limits of your car.

2. Look for smoke. When cars start skidding or spinning, the rubber on their tires burns. You'll never hear the screeching over the roar of your engine, but you'll be able to spot the burning rubber. Smoke ahead is the first sign of trouble.

3. Listen up! Each car has at least one crew member, equipped with binoculars and a two-way radio, stationed on a platform at the top of the grandstands. From there he can see the action all the way around the track unfolding as if on a game board. The spotter relays information to the driver and the pits, talking the driver around the course, even when everything's going right. Whether you see the wreck starting first or your spotter does, often your best hope is to follow the shouted words coming over your headset as the track is obscured in smoke.

When hell breaks loose at 190 mph.,
there's no room for error.

4. Be smooth. Don't get off the accelerator or on the brakes too abruptly. Doing so can cause your car to lose grip and spin, even without contact.

5. Look to the high side. Unless your spotter sees that the wreck is happening immediately around you, or that there are cars pinned against the outside wall, it is likely that he will instruct you to stay up—that is to steer toward the top of the banking, as a car that makes contact with the wall most often comes spinning back down across the track toward the infield.

6. Slow to go low. If your spotter does call for you to go low, or you see a gap there, steer down the banking. Slow as much as possible before your wheels hit the grass of the infield, as most of your steering and stopping power will be lost on the turf.

7. Assess the damage. Once through the wreckage, slow the car down, as the yellow caution flag will be out. Check the brakes and handling of your race car and listen for instructions from your spotter and your crew. Be aware of how close you are to the pit entrance, as most teams will bring their cars in for fuel and new tires during the caution period.

8. Take a deep breath. You made it. Now be sure to say something suitably laconic over the radio.

HOW TO PERFORM A BUMP-AND-RUN PASS

NASCAR legend Richard Petty likes to say that auto racing was invented "the day they made the second car." If that's the case, the "bump-and-run" was probably invented the day the second car got close enough to put its nose on the rear bumper of the first car.

Inelegant (some would say downright dirty), but effective as all get-out, the bump-and-run is what most of us would like to do now and then to that slowpoke in front of us on the freeway: Just tap him out of the way. Of course, trying that in the middle of morning rush hour would be against the law, not to mention irresponsible and extremely dangerous. On the racetrack, however, the move still has its place; it remains a tool to be used by professionals among professionals.

More specifically, it's a skill used in NASCAR, where the cars have sheet metal body work to absorb

"He could move you out of the way and you would be sitting there scratching your head and wondering, 'Did my car get loose, or did he hit me? I don't even know.'

— Four-time NASCAR champion Jeff Gordon on the bump-and-run prowess of the late Dale Earnhardt, Sr. (whose nickname, by the way, was "The Intimidator")

THE EXPERTS SPEAK

the contact. The tactic is usually confined to the short tracks (one mile or less), on which speeds aren't so high and contact is more common and less likely to lead to disaster. Still, the bump-and-run can often lead to heated words (or worse) in postrace confrontations between the drivers involved. NASCAR has not explicitly banned the move, however—as long as it isn't too blatant or doesn't lead to a wreck.

NASCAR vice president Jim Hunter has compared the situation to an umpire's judgment of the strike zone in baseball. "Almost every pitch is a judgment call by the umpire," Hunter told *The Greenville News.* "It's an awfully fine line, and we don't want to take the competition out of the sport."

Competition, of course, is just a fancy word for "tradin' paint." So, cinch up your belts and let's start competin'.

1. Assess your situation. Where are you in the field? How many laps are left in the race? How is your car handling? Do you have the machinery and the

FIG. A

time to work your way around the man in front of you, or is he holding you off? If two cars are racing equally fast, nose-to-tail in the closing laps of a race (Fig. A), the trailing driver will want to consider the bump-and-run pass. If there are a lot of laps left, it's better to wait—hopefully pit stops or changing track conditions will shake things up.

2. Assess your opponent. Take a lap or two to study how the driver ahead is approaching a corner: Note where he gets off the gas and where he begins to accelerate again. The best place for the bump-and-run is usually on the entrance to a corner, when the driver ahead is already at the edge of adhesion, his tires straining to keep the car in the groove.

3. Close the gap. On the entrance to the corner, go in a fraction harder than usual, letting your car come right up to his (Fig. B), the right side of your nose just

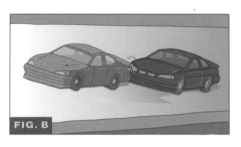

FIG. B

behind the left rear of his car. (NASCAR drivers normally run way closer together than your local driving instructor would recommend, but in this case, you're really going to get into his space.) You should not be squarely behind him, as this will not give you enough room to get around him and into the lead, even if he does slide to the side.

4. Throw the tap. With a little push, let the nose of your car make contact with the left rear of the car in front. This will cause the leader's rear tires to break loose, forcing him out of the groove and toward the outside of the track, where he will have to slow to avoid shooting into the wall (Fig. C).

FIG. C

5. Move with the groove. Still in the racing lane, you should have a clear shot ahead of you. Pass him on the inside and shoot past into the lead (Fig. D) just in time to take the checkered flag.

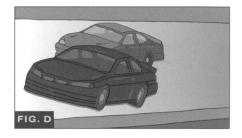

FIG. D

HOW TO PICK UP THE CORNER-PIN SPARE

Of all sports, bowling seems the simplest and most accessible. After all, we've all done it. According to the
American Bowling Congress (ABC), 70 million Americans
take to the lanes each year. And chances are that virtually
every one of those "keglers" has managed to roll a strike
or two. That's one of the great pleasures of the game: its
capacity to reward even the first-timer with success.
Surely, it seems, with just a little practice, you'd be knock-
ing 'em down every time.

But, of course, it's not that simple. And that's the other
great pleasure of the game: Sure, unlike golf, say, every
first shot in bowling is the same. But perfection is, while
attainable (for a game or two or even three), maddeningly
elusive. More than 3 million people bowl in sanctioned
league play in this country, and they will all tell you that
the most important factor in consistent high scoring is not
a crushing strike ball, but the ability to pick up your
spares. Bowlers call it "filling frames." Watch televised
tournaments and more often than not you'll see matches
being decided on open frames. That's why the pros practice relentlessly on all possible spare formations.

One of the most challenging spares—but one that to the
novice may appear simple—is the single corner pin. For a

right-handed bowler, it's the 10 pin (the one farthest right on the back row); for the lefty, it's the 7 pin (the one farthest left on the back row). And for even the most accomplished bowler, it's a test. Just ask Hall of Famer Mike Aulby. The brilliant lefthander, whose career included the 1979 PBA rookie of the year award as well as twenty-seven titles, was the top seed at the 1982 AMF Grand Prix in Paris but lost when he twice failed to convert on the 7 pin.

One reason the corner pin is so difficult is that there is only two-and-a-half inches of lane surface between the pin and the gutter, giving you about seven fewer inches to work with than on any other pin. So if you want to start filling frames, you better learn the proper approach.

1. Get your mind out of the gutter. The dropoff waiting just beyond the pin can be a formidable psychological obstacle. For that reason, focus on the pin, not on the abyss beyond.

2. Know your boards and arrows. Bowlers refer to the boards that make up the surface of the lane by numbers. The first board is the one right next to the gutter on the same side as your bowling arm; the 39th is the one right next to the opposite gutter. The arrows, marked on the surface, are five boards apart, with the first arrow on the fifth board, the second on the tenth, and so on. Line up on about the 35th board and aim to deliver the ball between the third and fourth arrows.

A cross-lane approach helps take the gutter out of play.

3. Think straight. Even if you roll a big hook on your strike ball, you want to roll the spare as straight as possible. One way to do this is to "break" your wrist backward throughout the delivery. Another is to adopt a "suitcase" grip, with your thumb on the inside, closer to your body, and your fingers on the outside. Adding speed to your delivery will also keep the ball from hooking.

4. Take a cross-lane approach. You will occasionally see beginning bowlers lining up on the same side of the lane as the pin (that is, a righthanded bowler to the extreme right side, a lefty to the extreme left), hoping to roll their ball straight down the edge of the lane to the pin. This approach leaves no margin for error, and almost always results in an open frame. Instead, line up at the opposite side of the lane from the pin.

5. Open your shoulders and square up to the target.

6. Don't worry about power. After all, you are only trying to knock over one pin. Concentrate on accuracy. Hit the pin flush. Now, go put that all-important mark on the score sheet.

How many times have you watched with horror as your first ball zeroes in a little too heavy on the head pin and, after a clatter of pins, found yourself staring at a 7-10 split—the dreaded goalposts of doom—thinking, "Well, I've got no chance." The fact is, you do have a chance—it just happens to be an almost infinitesimal one: Consider

GREAT MOMENTS IN SPORTS HISTORY

that in the more than forty years that Professional Bowlers Association tournaments have been airing on national television only three bowlers have converted a 7-10 split in televised competition. The last one to do it was Jeff Stayrook, in 1991. And those guys are pros.

Then again, according to the ABC record book, on October 4, 1999, one Victor Morra, rolling in a league game in Woodbridge, Connecticut, converted not one, but two 7-10 splits.

For a chance at such glory, don't try to shave the outside of the 10 (or 7) pin in an effort to send it across the lane to take out the other corner pin (the conventional approach). That won't happen. Your only hope is to drive one pin off the back wall with enough force that it rebounds into the other.

A better approach? Hit the pocket on your first ball.

BOXING

HOW TO THROW A LEFT HOOK

A good left hook is a thing of beauty—short, crisp, a matter of balance and timing more than brute force. The movement is a difficult one to learn, awkward at first, with its pivot and shift of weight. But once a fighter masters the hook, the punch often becomes his favorite, a faithful friend to turn to in times of need. The great Sugar Ray Robinson used to hook once, off the jab, and if he landed he just kept hooking—often as his opponent went down. (The single hook with which Robinson kayoed Gene Fullmer in 1957, by the way, should be preserved in a glass case at the Smithsonian—it was as perfect a punch as has ever been thrown.) Here's how to land a left hook of your own:

Joe Frazier, who honed his skills in the gyms—and, long before Rocky, *the slaughter-houses of Philadelphia— had as good a left hook as any in heavyweight history. "For me," Frazier always said, "it was always more like letting the hook go than actually throwin' it."*

LEGENDARY
SPORTS
HEROES

1. Start from a conventional boxing stance. Left foot forward, right back, about shoulder width apart, weight balanced evenly on the balls of both feet, with your whole body turned slightly to the right.

2. Hold your left arm out in front of you bent at about 90 degrees. Your fist should be level with your shoulder, thumb up. Your right arm should be cocked tightly at your side, fist protecting your chin (your opponent will be flinging hooks as well), elbow shielding your ribs. Keep your chin tucked behind a raised left shoulder. You don't want to be hit before you can get a punch off.

3. Begin your hook with a slight roll of your body to the left. Don't "telegraph" the punch by pulling back the elbow. The hook is not a looping blow.

Fist protecting chin

Chin tucked behind shoulder

Elbow shielding ribs

4. Pivot to the right on the ball of your left foot, the fist following in a tight arc. The elbow stays bent, the wrist rigid and the fist vertical. Your power comes through the shift of weight through the shoulder and hip. A classic left hook will travel little more than a foot.

HOW TO SURVIVE A NEAR KNOCKOUT

Muhammad Ali called it "the near room," the place a fighter goes when he has been rocked by a punch and is on the verge of being knocked out. He elaborated by saying, "It's dark, and there's snakes screaming and alligators playing the trombone, and they're calling you to come on in." And old time boxers just referred to this realm as "queer street." Clearly, this is a place no fighter wants to go. Yet every boxer—even the greatest, as Ali can attest—gets tagged now and then. It is how a fighter reacts in that moment of crisis, when his head is ringing and his legs have gone wobbly, that makes the difference between surviving the round and being counted out.

The most important thing is to buy time. Once wobbled by a punch, you are far more vulnerable to attack and far less able to withstand subsequent blows. For many fighters the immediate instinct when hurt is to strike back. But this is not the time for offense. You need

> **"If you get belted and see three fighters through a haze, go after the one in the middle. That's what ruined me—going after the other two guys."**
>
> **THE EXPERTS SPEAK**
>
> — Heavyweight champion Max Baer, after suffering a knockout loss

to clear your head and get your legs back—and avoid any additional damage in the process. Remember: live to fight another round.

There are two basic approaches. The first is to flee, to stay as far away from your opponent's fists as the 20-foot-square ring will allow, buying time to clear your head and make it to the bell. This strategy is often referred to as "getting on one's bicycle." To make like a pugilistic Lance Armstrong:

> **THE EXPERTS SPEAK**
>
> *"They stopped it too soon. It wasn't like I was disbobbulated."*
>
> — Carl "The Truth" Williams, after losing on a first-round TKO to Mike Tyson

1. Keep your gloves up beside your head. A fighter who has scored a knockdown or landed a big blow will have a tendency to charge in, loading up on big punches to the head in an effort to finish you off. You can't afford to let another blow land cleanly. Be prepared to roll with any punches that do make contact. Use your elbows to pick off blows to the body.

2. Circle away from your opponent's most dangerous hand. Do not move straight backward. If backed to the ropes, pivot quickly away and resume circling.

3. Use a quick, flicking jab to keep your attacker from setting up a big punch. Make sure to snap your fist back. This way, you'll avoid leaving yourself open for a counter punch.

If you can't run, hide—behind your raised gloves and elbows.

The second approach is counterintuitive, but in many cases even more effective: Get as close to your opponent as you can. Tie him up, smother him, get him into a clinch and don't give him room to punch. It means coming into range of the big guns, but once inside, you should be able to hold on long enough to ride out the barrage.

1. **Keep your gloves up.** When your attacker throws a punch, duck or slip under the glove and step in toward him, placing your left foot between his feet, denying him punching room and leverage.

2. **Place your arms around your opponent's elbows from the outside, pinning them against his ribs.**

3. **Lean as much of your weight as you can on your opponent.** Make him use his strength moving you around.

4. **Do not attempt to trade punches with your opponent.**

Finally, if you do succeed in surviving to the bell, use the one-minute rest period between rounds (assuming that wasn't the final round) to complete your recovery and to get instructions from your corner.

HOW TO HOLE OUT FROM THE SAND

The 17th hole on the Old Course at The Royal and Ancient Golf Club of St. Andrews is known as the Road Hole and is widely acknowledged as the hardest par four in golf. The hole gets its name from the stretch of blacktop lane that's in play behind the green, but the feature that makes the 17th so bloody treacherous is the pot bunker just beside the green, a deep, sandy hell that has swallowed the dreams of many a British Open contender. In the 1978 Open, Tommy Nakajima needed five tries to extricate himself—leading to the bunker's being dubbed "The Sands of Nakajima." In the 2000 Open, David Duval flailed away at the bottom of the Road Hole bunker, squandering a sure runner-up spot.

While the 17th at St. Andrews stands as the ultimate trial by sand for the pros (a move by the R&A in 2000 to reconfigure the bunker to make it less challenging was widely decried and quickly reversed), to many recreational golfers every sand shot looms like the Road Hole bunker. And every attempt to get up and down promises Nakajima-like humiliation. It needn't be that way. With the right approach and enough practice, you can develop the ability not only to get your ball consistently out of a trap, but also to leave it close to—and maybe even in—the hole.

1. Relax. You have a greater margin of error when playing from the sand than you do in any other situation, because you don't have to hit the ball—you just have to hit the sand a few inches behind the ball. So, don't let your mind dwell on what could go wrong. This should be one of your most comfortable and confident shots.

2. Open up. Your stance should be open (turned about 30 degrees to the left of the target line for a right-handed golfer), with the ball about two inches ahead of the midpoint of your stance.

3. Dig in. Work your feet into the sand for a firm foundation, with about 60 percent of your weight on your left foot.

4. Go weak. That is, grasp the club using a weak grip (rotating both hands counterclockwise so that—for a right-handed golfer—your left thumb will be on top of the club, pointing down the shaft). This will help you to keep the clubface open. Opening the clubface (that is, turning it out to aim to the right of the target) as much as 45 degrees allows it to bounce better through the sand and gives more loft to the ball.

5. Hang loose. Part of that "relax" idea again: Let your arms hang loose, with no tension. Bend your knees slightly and flex at the hips.

6. Don't aim at the ball. Aim for a spot anywhere from one to four inches behind the ball. If you want the

30°

toward the hole

To get out of a trap, just open it up—about 30 degrees.

ball to run after it hits the green (and it *will* hit the green), aim for a spot farther back, about three inches behind; if you want the ball to come out high and stop quickly on the green, hit about an inch behind the ball.

7. Swing it. Keeping the clubface open, swing the club along the line of your stance, accelerating through the shot. Many golfers stop their swing upon impact. Instead, concentrate on following through and finishing high.

THE EXPERTS SPEAK

Want some inspiration? Consider Lee Janzen's experience in the 2003 Memorial at Muirfield Village in Dublin, Ohio. The two-time U.S. Open champ finished second behind Kenny Perry and just ahead of Mike Weir, Tiger Woods, and Vijay Singh. And it was his sand play that kept Janzen in the hunt. Not once, not twice, but three times that weekend he holed out from a bunker. Of his third "golden ferret" (a term for the feat), a chip from the sand at the eighth hole that resulted in a birdie, Janzen said, "All I did was aim at the pin and hope it hit the pin, and it did. It went right in."

HOW TO HIT A KNOCKDOWN SHOT

Writing in *Sports Illustrated,* Jaime Diaz called the shot "a lightning bolt." And indeed the 140-yard eight-iron that Tiger Woods deposited 18 inches from the cup on the 36th hole of the 1995 U.S. Amateur at the Newport (R.I.) Country Club was as illuminating as any bolt from the blue. The shot—the kind of short "knockdown" iron that Woods hadn't had the year before, or in his Masters debut that spring—essentially sealed his match with Buddy Marucci, giving Woods his second U.S. Amateur title. More significant, it announced that Woods, at just 19 years of age, had elevated his game to a whole new level.

And Tiger knew it. "It showed how far my game has come," he told Diaz. "That shot at 18—Damn! That's the only shot I could hit close, that half shot. I didn't have it last year, I didn't have it at Augusta."

> **FOR YOUR INFORMATION**
>
> The Scots have a saying: "Nae wind, nae golf." That's why they invented the knockdown shot.

Most golfers never have it. The knockdown shot—sometimes called a half shot, a punch shot, or a Carnoustie (after the notoriously wind-whipped Scottish course)—is all about feel and touch. It allows a golfer to control distance, keep the ball low, and decrease spin. It is an invaluable weapon when you're faced with a strong headwind, or when you want to drive the ball under overhanging branches, or when you need to make a shot at a distance that's between clubs. Woods, of course, has gone on to expand his repertoire of knockdown shots almost infinitely, from his punched three-woods to his 118-yard knockdown pitching wedges. For all Tiger's prodigious length, it is his ability to hit the sort of resourceful, creative shots like the one he introduced at Newport that has allowed him to dominate the way he has.

You may never catch the sort of lightning in a bottle that Tiger regularly generates, but with some study and practice you can avoid having your score blown away with the wind. Here's how:

1. Go for more club. Take anywhere from one to three clubs more than you would hit with a full swing in calm conditions.

2. Sit in. Take a stance with your feet about shoulder width apart, with your weight more on your left foot, and "sit down," that is, bend your knees slightly more than normal.

3. Play back. The ball should be positioned well back in your stance. This will keep your hands ahead of the ball and ensure a lower trajectory.

4. Take aim. Your aim should be slightly left of the target, and your clubface should be square.

5. Keep your wrists "quiet." There should be no big release of your hands.

Swing easy and finish low to keep the ball down.

6. Swing easy. Many golfers try to hit harder into the wind, but this only lofts the ball more and increases spin. Instead, concentrate on taking an easy, three-quarter swing. Your hands should reach shoulder height on the backswing.

7. Finish low. Likewise on the finish, your hands should reach shoulder height. Your weight should be on your front foot, your chest facing the target.

HOW TO PUT BACKSPIN ON A SHORT IRON SHOT

Greg Norman knows how to spin a good tale. And a good golf ball. And sometimes the two come together.

Norman likes to tell the story of the time, back in the 1980s, when he was playing in the Italian Open and tournament organizers and sponsors had set up a promotional challenge: The first golfer to score a hole-in-one on one of the course's trio of par-threes would win a Lamborghini Countach. Norman, a confirmed speed-demon with a passion for Italian automobiles, had never driven a Lamborghini. He began thinking ace. He didn't get it on his first day, and neither did any of the other golfers. On the tournament's second day, Norman came to his first par-three on his second hole. He hit an eight iron that flew 15 feet past the flag, took a single hop, and then spun backward so that it—in Norman's words—"sucked back straight into the hole." Excited, the Shark finished his round and returned to the clubhouse, already revving the Countach in his mind, only to be informed that a young Italian club pro had aced one of the other par-threes ten minutes before Norman's backup hole-in-one. As a consolation prize, Norman received a leather carry-all.

Of course, Norman also had the consolation of a superb golf game that included the ability to hit such exquisite shots as that reversing eight-iron. Shots like that have earned Norman enough money (in lira, dollars, and every other denomination) to buy a fleet of Lamborghinis.

You may never get a crack at an Italian supercar, let alone score an ace to claim the keys, but the ability to land a golf ball and have it spin backward on the green can help you in crucial moments of a round. As Norman has written, "It's a wonderful shot to have, particularly when you're playing hard greens, or when you need to get close to a pin that's cut just beyond the lip of a front bunker."

Not to mention, it looks way cool—and is sure to draw some *oohs* and *ahs* from your playing partners.

1. Pick your shot. Assess the situation carefully before even attempting to spin the ball back. There's no need to try this shot if other approaches are available. But if you're aiming for a pin that's cut close to the front of the green, with little surface area to work with between the hole and the lip of a front bunker or a water hazard, definitely consider going in through the back door. Even then, don't try to make the shot if you're too far away—don't go for anything longer than a seven iron.

2. Assess your lie—and your landing. Don't try this from the rough. You need a clean, firm lie. The green should be firm (too hard and the shot won't bite; too wet and it will plug upon landing) and sloping toward you. In addition, it helps to hit the shot into the wind, which will help loft the ball. Don't try the shot with a tailwind, as it will cut the spin and run the ball forward after landing.

3. Know your ball. A wound balata ball with a thin cover will spin better than a ball with a solid center.

 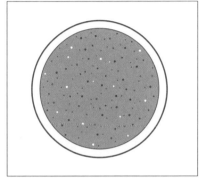

A glimpse inside a wound balata ball (left) and a ball with a solid center (right)

4. Start back. That is, play the ball a little back in your stance, a couple of inches behind your midline.

5. Hit clean. Strive to hit the ball crisply on the down-stroke, making contact with the ball first, not with the ground. This will "pinch the ball," driving it at impact into the turf and imparting maximum friction, and thus spin at launch.

6. Hit hard. Accelerate through the stroke. Club speed at impact determines the amount of spin. Your hands should be ahead of the ball at impact. Keep the clubhead low through the finish, taking a thin divot. If you've hit it right, all you need do is stand and listen for the "giant sucking sound," as the ball is drawn straight back to the hole.

Phil Mickelson has long been known for his masterful short game. On his approach shots he would often back up his golf ball so dramatically on the green that it seemed it should start blinking its tail lights and emitting a shrill "beep-beep-beep" sound. But going into the 2004 season Mickelson actually began to work on taking the spin off his short iron shots. "Everything was coming back 30, 40 feet," said Mickelson. "I couldn't get to the back pins. I couldn't get to tucked pins." The work paid off. At the Masters, Mickelson landed most of his approaches pin high and, even on Augusta's treacherous greens, they stayed put. Mickelson won his first major—and no one could accuse him of backing into it.

LEGENDARY SPORTS HEROES

GYMNASTICS

HOW TO PERFORM THE
THOMAS FLAIR

Listen to a gymnast describing his or her routine and it
sounds like roll call at the United Nations: Yurchenko.
Tsukahara. Diamadov. Watanabe. Unlike in most other
sports, the skills performed in gymnastics—from the most
arcane to the most spectacular—are often named after
famous athletes (usually the gymnast who invented the
skill or who first performed it in international competition). Interestingly, in a sport long dominated by East
European and Asian competitors, one of the most revolu-
tionary moves carries one of the most prosaic of names:
Thomas. The Thomas flair is one of the relatively few
moves in the International Gymnastics Federation Code of
Points to carry the name of an American gymnast.

Kurt Thomas was a five-time NCAA champion from
Indiana State University, the 1978 gold medalist on the
floor exercise, and one of the most decorated male gymnasts in U.S. history. Though he competed in the 1976
Montreal Games when he was just 20, Thomas was robbed
of his real chance at Olympic glory by the U.S.-led boycott
of the 1980 Games in Moscow. The average American may
not know Thomas, but chances are he or she knows the
move that he introduced to his sport and that was named
after him: In performing the Thomas flair a gymnast
swings his straddled legs in wide loops around his head

like the blades of a helicopter while supporting himself only on his rapidly dancing hands, pirouetting all the while.

What Thomas did was combine the two elements of a standard pommel horse routine—the split-leg scissors movement, normally swung on a vertical plane, with the gymnast's legs brushing the horse, and the circle, performed on a horizontal plane with the legs together—into one breathtaking sequence. Like all advanced gymnastics moves, the Thomas flair looks gloriously effortless when performed right, but actually requires years and years of skill-building and practice, as well as phenomenal upper-body strength. To perform the flair on the floor requires even more flexibility and dexterity. So, limber up and get ready to swing.

FIG. A

1. Hit the split. Assume a classic "splits" position (Fig. A), right leg straight out in front of you, left leg straight out behind, both legs flat on the floor. Your upper body should be perpendicular to the floor.

FIG. B

2. Lift it. Turn to your left, placing both hands, palms down, flat on the floor. Lean out over your hands, keeping your arms straight and firm, and elevate your legs. Raising your body weight onto your arms, bring your right leg—keeping it straight—in a sweeping clockwise motion to meet your left leg, bringing the two together behind you (Fig. B).

3. Circle it. Supporting yourself on your hands, swing both legs, about a foot or so off the ground, in a wide, flat circle clockwise. As your legs come around, lift your left arm to allow them to pass underneath (Fig. C). Place your left hand back down as quickly as possible after your legs have passed under.

4. Bring it around. Let your legs continue swinging around in front of you and under your right hand as you lift it and make a quarter turn to the right (Fig. D).

5. Think helicopter. As your legs pass behind you again, let them split as widely as possible, while still keeping them straight (Fig. E). With your legs straddled, continue to circle—

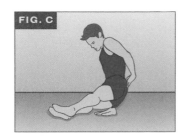

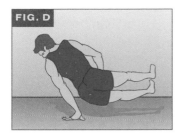

extending and swinging as much as possible from the shoulders (Fig. F). As your legs and hips pass under

each hand in turn, the leg on that side should be piked straight up next to your ear (Fig. G), while the opposite leg should extend directly down the body. Think smoothness and rhythm. In performing the Thomas flair, both are far more important than brute strength.

6. Bring it down. After a predetermined number of flared circles, let your momentum die and your right hand come down between your legs so that you return to the splits position, right leg forward, left leg behind (Fig. H).

Finally, after a quick hop to your feet, wait for a "10" from the judges—or, at least, the oohs and ahs of your friends.

HORSE RACING

HOW TO RIDE THE STRETCH AT THE KENTUCKY DERBY

They call the Kentucky Derby "the fastest two minutes in sports." It is also arguably the most exciting two minutes in sports. And the fastest and most exciting part of the Run for the Roses—which has taken place at Louisville's Churchill Downs every May for 130 years—comes in the homestretch, as the leaders thunder toward the finish and a victory that will give horse and jockey both a permanent place in racing history.

"Riders who have won the Derby—they have that in common," says Pat Day, who in 1992 guided Lil E. Tee to victory. "They can talk with each other about it, but no one else can really understand what it's like."

> **THE EXPERTS SPEAK**
>
> *"No matter how good you are or how many big races you've won, until you win the Derby, you're just another guy trying to."*
>
> — Steve Cauthen, 1978 winner aboard Affirmed.

When it comes to experience, Day, who was inducted into the Racing Hall of Fame in 1991, has as much as any jockey in history. A four-time Eclipse Award winner as outstanding jockey of the year, Day has won nearly 9,000 races in his career, including nine Triple Crown events. He is also the leading money winner of all time. As for the event we're discussing here, Day has ridden in twenty-two Kentucky Derbys.

"And every one is different," says Day. "The horse, the field, the conditions, nothing is ever the same. That's what makes it such a challenge."

Each horse has different strengths and weaknesses: Some are speed horses, eager and ready to run fast from the start. Others are strong finishers, capable of running off of the pace and then charging through in the final furlong. Trainers and jockeys spend months devising plans of attack for the race based on their horses' capabilities. A good rider will follow the plan to the letter—a great jockey will follow it and then find a way, in the thick of the race, to go just that little bit faster. For, late on that May Saturday afternoon, all that planning will take you only so far. When you bring your horse around to the quarter pole, with a mile gone and only that wide straightaway to go, and those thousands of fans on their feet and roaring as one, you had better be in position and ready to ride your heart out.

1. **Breathe.** "I'm happy to say that the body responds without us having to think about it," says Day, "because otherwise there'd be a whole lot of us falling off the horse, passed out from complete lack of oxygen." Relaxation is key. From the moment you and your mount burst from the starting gate, you will have been up off the saddle, balanced on the balls of your feet in the irons, and crouched over the horse's withers (the ridge between his shoulder blades). But it is important

during the first part of the race that you keep the horse at ease through your posture and grip—and also keep yourself from becoming too fatigued. You should be "sitting back" a little, not right up on the horse's neck. Says Day, "I've found that when I'm comfortable, the horse is."

2. Assess your position and the state of the field.
At the half-mile pole (that is, with a half mile to go to the finish), you should have a sense of which horses are still contending: who's tiring, who's coming on strong, who's still running easy. Unless you're on a speed horse and have been trying to win it from the front, you'll want to get into position now.

3. Don't get boxed in.
The 1999 edition of the race has been called "the Demolition Derby," as banging and jostling in that year's 19-horse field left many possible winners out of contention. Don't get caught up in a game of bumper cars. To get around other horses, change lanes, just as you would on a freeway, without reining in the horse.

FOR THE RECORD

In United States racing, including the Kentucky Derby, there are few rules regarding a jockey's use of the whip. Some racing observers have begun to push for regulations to prevent jockeys from whipping a horse excessively, or when the horse is no longer in contention.

4. Call on your horse.
You will have been holding him back, keeping him relaxed until this point. Now let him know that the race is on.

When it's time to go, jockeys urge their mounts on with whips and kisses.

5. Shorten up your grip on the reins. You should be closer to his neck and pushing down on his head.

6. Get lower over his withers. Bend over more so that your back is parallel to the horse's.

7. Urge him on. Day encouraged Lil E. Tee with quick little air kisses. "Kind of a smooching sound in his ear," says Day. Some jockeys will go to the whip at this point.

8. Keep running for the wire. "I remember that when we came to the $1/8$ pole and only Casual Lies was ahead, I knew that we were not only in position to win, but that we were going to win," says Day of his stretch run in '92. "This indescribable feeling started way down deep inside, but I didn't let it erupt until after we passed the finishing pole."

The fastest time for the Kentucky Derby was set by the great Secretariat in 1973 at 1 minute, 59 $2/5$ seconds. The slowest winning time for the 1 $1/4$ mile distance was Stone Street's 2:15 $1/5$ in 1908. As Day says, every race is different. And within every race, things change in a heartbeat—or a hoofbeat.

FOR THE RECORD

SKATING

HOW TO PERFORM A QUAD JUMP

Conventional wisdom says that the hardest thing to do in all of sports is to hit a baseball. (It's the whole "round ball with a round bat" thing.) And, sure enough, in 2003 when *USA Today* published its "definitive" list of the top-ten most difficult sports skills (determined with the help of experts and scientists), hitting a baseball ranked No. 1. But it's worth noting that in an online poll of readers conducted in conjunction with the series, landing a quad jump in figure skating (ranked No. 6 by the editors) came in first—and with no help from the French judges.

The best figure skaters, like the best gymnasts and divers, create an illusion of effortlessness, their most spectacular moves performed with such precision and grace that it's easy for a spectator to forget just how difficult what they're watching really is. And all those sequins and the swelling music and the roses and the hugs at the end tend to obscure the sweat and focus and sheer athleticism involved in performing a competitive skating program. But when it comes to the quad, the *USA Today* readers had no illusions: Launching yourself a foot and a half or more off the ice to perform four rotations in the air in about a half a second before landing back on the ice on the thin edge of a steel blade is clearly very, very hard to do.

The first American to land a quad in international competition was 17-year-old Timothy Goebel at the 1998 International Skating Union Junior Series Final in Lausanne, Switzerland. A year later Goebel became the first skater ever to complete three quads in one program. Dubbed the Quad King, he went on to win the bronze medal at the 2002 Winter Olympics. (The first female skater to land a quad in competition was 14-year-old Miki Ando of Japan, who wowed the crowds at the 2002 Junior Grand Prix Final in The Hague, Netherlands.) Goebel has said that, for him, the quad has become "just another jump."

Right. And a Randy Johnson fastball under the chin is just another pitch to hit.

(Note: These instructions are for a skater who spins clockwise—a right-handed skater; for a left-handed skater they would simply be a mirror image.)

1. Build speed. Skate forward on your left foot, left leg bent at the knee, right leg extended out behind you, skate just off the ice (Fig. A). Your arms should be extended out to your sides, hands about waist high. You will be using them to create your spin.

FIG. A

2. Rotate. Make a quarter turn to your right (rotating

clockwise). You should be on the back outside edge of your left skate, your right leg sweeping low around to the right.

3. Pick it. Stab the ice with the toe pick of your right skate. This will launch you into the jump (Fig. B).

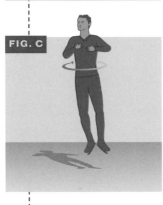

4. Spin it. Draw both hands tight into your body, arms bent at the elbow, right arm above the left. Your head should be up and turned to the right, into the twist, your legs straight and held tightly together (Fig. C). Pull everything in tight to your vertical axis to increase rotation.

5. Open up. As you complete the fourth rotation (after 0.5 seconds), let your arms come out from your body with the elbows rising almost to shoulder height to slow your rotation and steady yourself for landing (Fig. D). Let your legs separate and reach for the ice with your left skate. Your right leg, bent at the knee, should complete the final circle to extend behind you as you land on the back outside edge of

your left skate, facing forward
(Fig. E).

6. Sell it. With your arms raised,
palms down, your head up and
facing forward, and your right leg
held up behind you, glide on with
a big smile on your face.

Expect some roses and some
hugs when you come off the ice. Cry if you feel like it.

*Three of figure skating's main jumps are named after their orig-
inators. Axel Paulsen of Norway landed the first
single Axel in 1882. Ulrich Salchow, a ten-time
world champion from Sweden, launched his
namesake in 1909. And Alois Lutz of Austria
introduced the single Lutz in 1913.*

**LEGENDARY
SPORTS
HEROES**

TENNIS

HOW TO DELIVER A CRUSHING SERVE

A comparison: Monza, Italy, 2003—Michael Schumacher sets the record for the fastest Formula One race, piloting his Ferrari to victory in the Italian Grand Prix at an average speed of 153.841 mph. Delray Beach, Florida, 2004—Andy Roddick sets a record for the fastest tennis serve, booming an ace past Sweden's Jonas Bjorkman in a Davis Cup match at 152 mph.

While it may be comparing apples and, well, tennis balls, the image of Roddick's serve streaking toward you at more or less the same velocity as Schumacher's screaming red Ferrari paints a pretty vivid picture of what it's like to face the most powerful serve in modern tennis.

For many recreational players, the serve can too easily become a liability, as they either fail to control it, leading to double faults, or—in making sure the serve clears the net—they offer up a slow floater to their opponent. In contrast, a big serve can go a long way toward strengthening your game. It is, of course, the stroke that begins every point, and it is also the one shot over which you have total control. There's nothing like winning a point with one swing. Or at least setting yourself up with placement and pace for a quick win. Powerful servers such as Roddick, Pete Sampras, Goran Ivanisevic, or Lindsay Davenport have the upper hand, in fact, from the moment their hand goes up to toss the ball for a serve.

Remember, though, that an increase in power can lead to a sacrifice of control. Among the pros, the big servers generally hope to get their first serves in about 60 percent of the time. Anything less requires some tweaking or backing off the firepower.

Finally, you need not be a giant to develop a powerful serve. As former pro player turned TV analyst Mary Carillo says, "Timing, not body size, is the key to power." Sampras, after all, was an unimposing 6'1", and look what he did. So, if you're looking to supercharge your serve—if not quite to the Roddick-Schumacher neighborhood, then at least to a point that puts a little fear in the eyes of your weekend opponent—grab a racket and get busy. Because they do not serve who stand and wait.

> *Many experts believe Pancho Gonzalez had the greatest serve in tennis history. Not only was Gonzalez's serve power-ful, but it was also smooth and relaxed enough that it remained as effective in the fifth set as it was in the first. "Your serv-ice," said Pancho, "usually determines whether you will win or lose a match."*

LEGENDARY SPORTS HEROES

---

1. Relax. Remember, you are in control. Let the power come from a smooth, fluid stroke. Don't start by tens-ing up and thinking, "I'm going to smash this one!"

FIG. A

2. Feel your foundation. It is crucial to begin from a well-grounded, well-balanced stance (Fig. A). Much of the power of your serve will come from your legs and hips. Your feet should be about shoulder width apart. Position your front foot at a 30- to 40-degree angle to the baseline. Your back foot should be parallel to the baseline, and your weight should be over your back foot. Bend at the knees as you initiate the toss.

3. Time the toss. Make the toss with your arm out to the side of your body—not directly in front—as this will force your shoulders to rotate and help to initiate power. If you're right-handed, make your toss slightly to the right, about one o'clock (if you're a lefty, aim for 11 o'clock), as this will put the ball directly above your hitting shoulder.

4. Think height. Throw the ball slightly higher than the point at which your racket will strike it. Throwing too low will limit your extension and thus your power.

5. Coil for power. This is the position that generates your oomph (Fig. B). Your throwing

FIG. B

arm will be fully extended and to the side of your body, causing your shoulders to rotate and tilt (front shoulder up). Your hips should rotate forward. Your knees will be bent, storing energy for the explosion into the ball. Your head should be up. Your grip should not be too tight, and your arm should feel loose and free. Do not try to muscle the shot. The palm of your racket hand should be facing in, toward the side of your head.

6. Blast off. Drive upward into the stroke (Fig. C). Your legs should straighten, propelling you off the surface of the court. Contact the ball at the highest point in your swing, snapping your wrist forward and pronating it (so that the palm rotates to the outside).

FIG. D

7. Go ahead and grunt. Exhale strongly at the moment of impact. Holding your breath only builds up tension and robs you of power. And be sure to keep your eye on the ball (Fig. D), because sometimes even the most crushing serves will be returned.

HOW TO HIT THE DROP SHOT

Sports Illustrated tennis writer Jon Wertheim has also covered some boxing in his day, which may explain his occasional use of the fistic metaphor when describing the presumably more genteel battles waged on the court. Consider his report from the 2002 French Open: "Drop shots are the body blows of tennis," Wertheim wrote after watching Serena Williams win the second set against Russian teenager Vera Zvonareva with a beautifully set-up and masterfully disguised example of the shot, which died in the dirt of Roland Garros stadium and left Zvonareva staggered. "They might not elicit the *oohs* and *aahs* from fans seated ringside, but they can inflict just as much damage."

The analogy is a particularly apt one. Tennis in the modern era is increasingly dominated by the big hitters, the racket-wielding counterparts of boxing's headhunting heavyweights. Certainly on grass and asphalt they rule. But on a clay court, a player with a good drop shot can, like a savvy boxer with a well-timed hook or uppercut to the ribs, sap his opponent's power and set him up for the knockout.

> **TRAINING TIP**
>
> *To develop the soft touch necessary for an effective drop shot, practice tossing a ball into the air and catching it on the strings of your racket without any bounce.*

The drop shot is a short, soft shot, hit with spin, either forehand or backhand, that just clears the net and bounces twice before your opponent can reach it. It is a particularly effective weapon against a player who doesn't come up to the net well. Don't use the drop shot as a defensive ploy—make it a quick, surprising offensive move. An effective drop shot will add punch to your game. Just ask Andy Roddick or Andre Agassi, two players who've used the move with great success (see call-outs below).

1. Pick the spot for your shot. Set up your opponent for a drop shot by moving him back behind the baseline, and to one side of the court or the other, with a series of deep, forceful shots. It's worth noting, too, that the drop shot is much more effective if hit into the wind.

2. Get a baseline reading. That is, position yourself just inside the baseline.

In an April 2004 Davis Cup quarterfinals match between the U.S. and Sweden, Andy Roddick beat Jonas Bjorkman 7-6(3), 6-4, 6-0, clinching a win for the United States. After losing that first set, Roddick roared back to take the match. He was, he said, "in the zone." In the third set he hit a particularly brilliant drop shot, after which team captain Patrick McEnroe remarked to him, "I didn't know you have that shot." Replied Roddick, "I didn't either, but don't tell anybody else."

THE
EXPERTS
SPEAK

FIG. A

3. Get a grip. Most players use the Eastern grip (also known as the shakehands grip), in which you grip the racquet as if shaking hands (Fig. A), for both the forehand and the backhand drop shot. You should play the backhand drop shot one-handed.

4. Disguise your intentions. Don't telegraph your shot. Begin the drop shot with a short backswing, taking the racket back about two feet and up about a foot from the point at which you intend to make contact with the ball (Fig. B).

FIG. B

5. Tilt. Angle the face of your racquet back about 30 to 50 degrees.

FIG. C

6. Think "short and sweet." With a short, gentle motion, hit down across the ball, bending at the knees and moving the shoulder and elbow while keeping the wrist firm (Figs. C, D, E). Watch the ball travel all the way to your racket.

7. Spin, spin, spin. By brushing downward across the ball you impart lift and spin to the ball. A well-struck

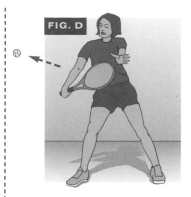 

drop shot should just clear the net and bounce twice before your opponent can race forward to retrieve it. A well-struck drop shot can even spin back toward you.

> *There are few craftier old warriors than Andre Agassi. At the 2003 U.S. Men's Clay Court Championships in Houston, the 32-year-old Agassi faced 20-year-old Andy Roddick, the rocket-serving young gun of American tennis. Roddick had come out slugging and taken the first set 6-3, and was leading 2-0 in the second, with Agassi serving at love-40. That was when the old master employed a bit of tennis's version of the sweet science. Agassi hit a bold backhand drop shot from the baseline that froze Roddick, won the point, and turned the tide of the match. Playing with superb focus and using every weapon in his arsenal, Agassi went on to win the set 6-3, and took the third 6-4 (winning the fifth game on another drop shot). It was a stunning demonstration of what a well-timed drop shot can do.*

GREAT MOMENTS IN SPORTS HISTORY

TABLE TENNIS

HOW TO PUT SPIN ON THE SERVE

Remember the rules? No smashes because the ceiling was too low. Anything that landed in the laundry hamper was a do-over. And, of course, whoever was ahead when Mom called you up for supper won that game. That was more or less how millions of us grew up playing Ping-Pong. (If the table you played on was outside at your summer camp, there were probably rules about rain delays. If it was in the den of your frat house, well, there were probably no rules at all.)

World-class competitive table tennis bears about as much resemblance to those basement back-and-forths as an aria by Pavarotti does to your singing in the shower. Since Richard Nixon's so-called Ping-Pong Diplomacy in the 1970s introduced the best Chinese players to television, it has become clear to most of us that this is one fast and furious sport, and that the pros are doing things with their paddles and that little ball that sometimes seem to defy the laws of physics.

> **The top players can put 9,000 rpm of spin on a ball.**
>
> *FOR YOUR INFORMATION*

Watch Jan-Ove Waldner, for instance. The multiple world and Olympic champion—who long since transcended sports to become a veritable pop idol in his native Sweden—has been described as the Pelé, the Michael Jordan, and the Wayne Gretzky of table tennis. A wizard at every facet of the game ("When he is playing good," said one opponent, "he seems to know what you are thinking. When he is playing very good, he seems to know what the ball is thinking."), Waldner has always had a serve that is particularly mind-blowing. With a three-foot-high toss of the ball, from behind a rolled shoulder, and a seemingly limp service hand, he completely camouflages the contact point of the serve and the degree of spin he is imparting to the ball, leaving his opponent no option but to wait and react. In this way, Waldner has always controlled the pace and direction of his points.

You may never develop the "be-the-ball" mastery of a Waldner (who, after all, began playing at age six, when only his paddle was visible over the edge of the table), or of any of the spectacular Chinese players who still dominate the world rankings. But, with a little work on a more sophisticated serve, who knows? You may find yourself ruler of the rec room.

1. Be a surface thinker. The type of rubber on the surface of your paddle will determine the amount of spin you'll be able to put on the ball. (You can, and most players do, use different rubber on each side of the paddle, but since 1983 the rules require that the different rubbers be of different colors.) A thicker rubber creates more power and spin. A "pips-out" surface—that is, one studded with tiny pimples—increases control on your shot, but cuts spin. A "pips-in" surface—or "inverted rubber"—creates more spin and greater speed.

2. Shake hands. With your paddle, that is. While the pen hold grip (a revelation when those first Chinese showed up on TV) and the Seemiller grip (in which the index finger is extended along the side of the paddle) are still used, the traditional shakehands grip has increasingly become the grip of choice among all players. Simply grasp the paddle as if you were shaking hands, with your index finger rested across the bottom of one side of the blade and your thumb just along the bottom of the other side. Your middle, ring, and pinkie finger should be around the handle. This grip gives you maximum flexibility and versatility.

3. Go fore it. Top players generally prefer forehand serves, as they allow you to launch an immediate attack on your forehand side. Begin from the left-hand corner of your side of the table. Stand perpendicular to the table, with your feet about shoulder width apart, your left foot close to the corner. Your left shoulder should be slightly lowered and closed and pointing toward your opponent (Fig. A).

FIG. A

4. Toss it. With your left hand, throw the ball from an open palm to about eye level or higher. The higher the toss, the more action will be imparted to the ball, but the less control you'll have.

FIG. B

5. Keep it close. With the back of your blade up, nearly perpendicular to the floor, and your wrist fairly firm, sweep the blade across the back of the ball (Fig. B). Your forearm should stop at your ribs, at which point—as you strike the ball—your wrist should curl up and in toward your chest (Fig. C). This will deliver top sidespin to the ball, making it very hard for your opponent to read the serve and return it.

FIG. C

6. Mix it up. As you become proficient with the serve, vary the height of your toss and the target of the serve. In time you'll also be able to create underspin by altering the angle of your paddle.

HOW TO THROW THE JAVELIN

There are few sights in sports as majestic as a great
javelin throw. From the instant of explosive release, the
eye follows the arc of the spear as it soars, high and hum-
ming, seemingly the length of the entire stadium, to its
piercing touchdown in the turf. It is an arc that spans all
the way back to the ancient Olympic Games of 708 B.C., a
throwback, if you will, to the heroes and gods of antiquity.
After all, unlike most sporting implements, the javelin is,
in its essence, a weapon. The business end was originally
meant for animals or enemy soldiers, not for scurrying
officials with tape measures. (The javelin remains a
potentially dangerous event, banned by some high school
federations; certainly no one on the infield should turn his
or her back on the thrower!)

The modern javelin is constructed of three parts: the
shaft, the head and the grip. The shaft originally was made
of solid wood—traditionally olive. In 1953, however,
Franklin "Bud" Held, a three-time NCAA javelin champ
from Stanford, invented a hollow shaft that made the spear
far lighter and more aerodynamic. Now all javelins feature
a hollow steel shaft, a metal head, and a grip formed of
wound cord. Men compete with a javelin that measures
between 2.60 and 2.70 meters (between about 8´6˝ and
8´10˝) and weighs 800 grams; women with one that measures between 2.20 and 2.30 meters (between about 7´2˝ and

7'6") and weighs 600 grams. Traditionally, throwers have used a running, overhand toss, but in the 1950s Felix Erausquin of Spain introduced a spinning technique similar to a discus thrower's and began launching the javelin more than 300 feet. The International Amateur Athletic Federation, the sport's worldwide governing body, quickly banned the "Spanish Style," as it was unpredictable and dangerous. (An errant spin release could send the javelin off at a wild angle.) The 300-foot barrier would not be exceeded again until the 1980s.

In 1986 the IAAF moved the center of gravity in the men's javelin forward 10 cm, making the nose drop more quickly, cutting down on flat landings—which were dangerous and difficult to measure—and once again limiting the lengths of throws, which were threatening to soar right out of the infield. In 2001 the same modification was made in the women's javelin. Despite all the tinkering, the javelin remains track and field's highest- (and longest-) flying event.

> *Okay, maybe we can't think of any legendary javelin throwers. But here are three javelin throwers who, chances are, you never knew threw the javelin: actor Michael Landon, NFL quarterback Terry Bradshaw, and country music star Garth Brooks.*

LEGENDARY SPORTS HEROES

1. Clear the area! Make sure the throwing area is clear on all sides and that the landing zone is also clear. Unless you are in competition, retrieve your own spear. If you are throwing with others, you should all retrieve your javelins at the same time. No throwbacks. And no catching, either!

2. Stay between the lines. The approach runway is 4 meters wide and 30 meters long and ends in a curved line from behind which all throws must be made. To be counted as fair, throws must land within the throwing sector, a v-shaped area of 29 degrees coming out from the end of the runway.

3. Palm it. Grip the javelin by placing it diagonally across your palm, with your middle finger hooked over the back of the cord grip. Your index finger may curl around the shaft, or lie along it. Do not clasp the shaft too tightly.

4. Think speed. The key to the throw is to get the javelin moving as fast as possible, and at the optimum angle, straight through the point of release. A big part

Brute strength is far less important to a javelin

of generating this speed comes on your approach run. Don't think of it as an all-out sprint, though. Speed is important, but only as long as you can control it. Run with the javelin held just above your head, parallel to the ground, accelerating into your final five-step approach.

5. Hit your marks. You should hit your check-mark step on your left foot. As your right foot comes forward, with toe turned out at a 45-degree angle, your right arm should start back. Your left arm should be held out in front of you. Step forward onto your left foot, which should be turned slightly to the right, beginning to align the body for the final rotation. As the right foot comes forward for the cross step, your body should turn to the right.

6. Plant and pull. Plant your left foot and pull in your left arm. Your left leg should come down quickly and straight. Your body, from your right toe to your right

throw than controlled speed and timing.

arm—at its farthest point back—should form a bow shape. Pull the javelin into the throw, leading with your elbow. (Do not snap the arm.) Release the javelin at about a 30-degree angle. Your follow-through should carry you onto your left foot just in front of the foul line. Finally, feel free to give an enormous grunt—in Finnish, if possible—at the moment of release.

HOW TO POLE VAULT

Pole vaulters are the wild men (and women) of track and field. To excel as a vaulter requires a sprinter's speed, a diver's agility, and the upper-body strength of a gymnast. Oh, yeah, it also helps to have a total disregard for the dangers inherent in flinging oneself 15 to 20 feet off the ground. You have to want to fly. Or at least to swing on a vine. One of the greatest vaulters of all time, 1960 Olympic champ Don Bragg, went by the nickname of "Tarzan" and unleashed a king-of-the-jungle yell while on the medal stand in Rome. It's a wonder, really, that Bragg's bellow hasn't become a tradition for all pole vaulting champions.

Pole vaulting—the only event in track and field in which the implement propels the athlete, not the other way around—seems to have originated in Europe as a way to cross canals too wide to be jumped. In the late nineteenth century the practice evolved (as so many do) into a sport, and the objective became height rather than distance. The first competitive poles were made from bamboo, and athletes jumped on grass without mats to land on. The winning height at the first modern Olympic Games, in Athens in 1896, was a dizzying 10 feet, 6 inches. It has been up, up, and away ever since.

Safety is a crucial consideration in pole vaulting. The original grass and sand landing sites have long since given way to substantial cushioning areas known as pits. The padding is positioned not just where a vaulter is supposed to land, but also anywhere he or she might end up in the event of a botched vault or a snapped pole. In addition, some vaulters have experimented with helmets, though the extra weight and bulkiness pose a problem.

The key to a successful jump is the conversion of the vaulter's speed down the runway into energy in the pole with as little waste as possible. A heavier vaulter will generally use a stiffer pole than a lighter vaulter in order to get the same degree of bend.

RULES OF THE GAME

Dave Volz, a top American vaulter in the 1980s, had an uncanny ability to reach out in midair and replace the cross bar if he dislodged it during a vault. The practice, which became known as "Volzing the bar," is now against the rules.

To perfect their technique, vaulters perform a variety of exercises and drills (using swings and ropes and other gymnastics apparatus) in addition to repeated vaults.

So, grab a pole and head down to the far end of the runway. Like a jumbo jet, you're going to need some room to take off.

1. Make your mark. Get close enough to a pole vault runway during a meet or practice, and you will notice little strips of tape, marked with different colors or initials, stuck to the edge of the running surface. These are the various vaulters' starting points for their approach runs. You will want to measure your runup down to the inch so that you can consistently hit your plant spot at top speed without lunging or chopping your steps. If you find that you're still accelerating at the plant, move the starting point back. If you're struggling to maintain top speed, move the starting point up.

2. Pick up sticks. Your pole, that is. During the approach run, the pole (for a right-handed vaulter) should be held on the right side, with your top hand (that is, your right hand, which will be higher on the pole at vertical) close to your right hip, loosely gripping the pole. Your palm will be facing up, thumb to the rear. Your left hand should be out in front, palm down, with a solid grip on the pole. The pole should be pointing upward at about a 45-degree angle.

3. Punch it. Accelerate quickly, running with an upright posture. Your feet should make quick, "punching" steps over the ground.

4. Plant it. Two steps before takeoff, the pole tip should come to the ground (Fig. A). One step before takeoff the upper end of the pole should be rising beside your face. At the takeoff step, the pole should be "planted" in the box at the end of the runway, directly under the bar. Your arms should be fully extended and locked overhead, with your left, or "plant," foot directly under your top hand. Do not

FIG. A

FIG. B

FIG. C

FIG. D

FIG. E

FIG. F

collapse or bend your arms, as this will dissipate the momentum generated by your sprint.

5. Be the "C." At takeoff, your right leg, bent at a 45-degree angle, should drive up, while you power off of your fully extended left leg. Your position, from your right arm down to your left toe, should form a "C" shape (Fig. B).

6. Rock and row. As the pole flexes, swing your trail leg in a large arc to generate the "rock back" motion. Your arms, still fully extended and locked, should make a vigorous "rowing" motion, sweeping down as your legs come up, so that your bottom (left) arm is parallel with your legs, your hand even with your knees (Fig. C). At this point your left arm should bend.

7. Climb the pole. As the pole moves to vertical, you should make a quarter turn around the pole and, upside down, begin to travel up the pole (Fig. D). Be sure to move vertically and not out toward the pit; allow the pole to shoot you upward.

8. Take it over the top. Make another quarter turn, pushing into a handstand position, at the peak of which you will jackknife over the bar, facing downward and pushing off from the pole (Fig. E).

9. Take a fall. Drop backward, arms and legs spread, to land on your back in the pit (Fig. F).

part *THREE*
EXTREME
sports

CLIFF-DIVING

HOW TO CLIFF-DIVE

Everything is extreme these days. Extreme skiing. Extreme climbing. Extreme fighting. Extreme makeovers. But, for all their Lycra-clad lunacy and amped-up attitude, have any of today's Gen-Extremers ever really matched the sheer *cojones* of those original extreme athletes, the cliff-divers of Acapulco? Remember those old *Wide World of Sports* episodes, black-and-white footage from the impossibly exotic setting of . . . Mexico? Sun-bronzed young men in their tiny swim trunks climbing the rugged cliffs and then swanning off the bluffs, out beyond the deadly rocks into the churning surf of the Pacific?

It all seems so dated now, so '60s, so Jet-Age. Where's the Red Bull and the Blink 182 soundtrack? Where's the sign-age and the celebrity judges? Where's the 'tude? But wait just a minute—hold your halfpipe. Think about what these guys were doing (are doing, for the divers are still per-forming today): These young men, known as *clavadistas,* perform their daring feats from the top of the cliffs known as La Quebrada, a dramatic rock formation on the western coast of Acapulco. From the top, it is a 130-foot plunge to the sea. That would be formidable enough into a nice, deep swimming pool. But two factors make the diving at La Quebrada so daunting. The first is the roll of the surf. Only when the waves wash into the narrow gorge below the cliffs is there enough water to protect a diver. Mis-time your plunge and you will hit the rocks below the surface. The second factor is the cliff itself. Divers must clear nearly 30 feet of outcropping to hit the water. There are no do-overs on the cliffs of Acapulco. With tourists and aficionados watching from the bar of the nearby El Mirador hotel and from a small rocky terrace across from the bluffs, the clavadistas take the plunge several times each day and evening, finishing the spectacle with a nighttime dive holding flaming torches.

The authorities in Acapulco make sure that no tourists get too brave and attempt the dive. But should you somehow find yourself atop La Quebrada someday, you'll want to know just what to do—and not just let things fall where they may.

1. Suit up. No jammies or oversize swim trunks here. You want a nice tight suit that's going to be aerodynamic on the way down—and stay on when you hit the water.

2. Heads up. At La Quebrada, what comes down must first go up. You will need to free-climb the brown and gray bluffs on your way to the various jumping-off points, which range from less than 50 to 130 feet above the Pacific. You will be climbing barefoot and without the aid of ropes or railings. Take your time and follow the paths of the experienced divers. Climb slowly and deliberately; you will want to be fresh when you reach the top.

3. Settle up. With your god, that is. There is a small, sky blue shrine atop La Quebrada, at which the divers will customarily stop to pray. It may be part of the show for the crowd at El Mirador, but then again, what could it hurt?

4. Timing is everything. The clavadistas ply their trade only at high tide, when there is enough water in the thin gorge below the bluffs. Even then, however, you must time your dive so that you hit the surface when an incoming wave has raised the level of water in the inlet to its highest point. This means that you must start your plunge when the gorge appears far from full. It is a frightening prospect—but watch the experienced divers and you'll see that there is no other safe approach.

5. Far out, man. First rule of successful diving? You must reach the water. That is, your dive must carry you out beyond the slope of the cliff. You have a lot of vertical room to play with, but you must still initiate a strong forward propulsion. From an erect standing position, feet together, arms raised straight above your head, bend at the knees. Bring your arms down and back at hip level and then sweep them forward and out as you drive forward with your legs.

6. Lay it out. Arch your back, with your body parallel to the water, your arms spread straight out. Let gravity bring you forward into a vertical position. At this point, bring your arms together over your head, right hand in a fist, with the left locked over it.

Leap straight out, with your body parallel to the water. Gravity will bring you forward into a vertical position.

7. Keep it straight. Enter the water perfectly perpendicular. After entering, spread your arms and arch your back to keep yourself from going too deep. Once you surface, give a quick wave and accept the applause (and possibly the tossed coins) from the watching tourists.

GREAT MOMENTS IN SPORTS HISTORY

The 1963 film Fun in Acapulco *featured Elvis Presley as a deckhand in Mexico who gets fired and turns to cliff-diving. The film introduced countless Americans to the wonders of this sport. Alas, the King did not perform his own stunts.*

HOW TO COMPLETE A LUGE RUN

For competitors in the sport of luge, life is one big snow day. Just ask Fred Zimny. The manager of recruitment and development for USA Luge, the sport's national governing body, Zimny grew up in New Jersey, sledding on less than inspiring hills. Watching the 1976 Winter Olympics in Innsbruck, Austria, on television, the young Zimny became fascinated with the luge. That summer, driving to Montreal with his father to see the Summer Games, he stopped in Lake Placid, New York, then the site of the only luge run in the U.S. It has been, well, all downhill since. A national competitor for many years, Zimny has gone on to head up USA Luge's Slider Search program, which since 1985 has been introducing the sport to prospective athletes through clinics and demonstrations across the country.

"There's no reason that a kid in, say, Dallas can't be as good a luge athlete as a kid who grows up in Lake Placid," says Zimny. "They just need the exposure."

To that end, the Slider Search program teaches young-sters age 11 to 14 the basics of riding a luge and gives them a chance to take a run down a paved course on a sled equipped with wheels. The most promising athletes are invited to Lake Placid or to Park City, Utah, to try the real thing. The program has already borne fruit. Brian

Martin, a 1998 Olympic bronze and 2002 Olympic silver medalist, was discovered at a Slider Search in 1987, as were six other members of the 2002 Olympic team.

There are currently thirteen artificially refrigerated luge tracks throughout the world. On these tracks men's runs are between 1,300 and 1,500 meters long; women's are 800 to 1,200. All tracks are different in their layout but all require sliders to negotiate a series of banked curves at speeds often exceeding 80 mph. "The fear factor is there for beginners," says Zimny. "But for national- and world-class sliders, the guys who can keep calm and cool are the ones who succeed."

Lying on your back and sliding 80 mph down a mountain? What could be cooler?

1. Suit up. It's obviously cold on the ice, but sliders dress for speed, not warmth. You'll be sporting light-weight long underwear beneath a full-body speedsuit, which zips up the back and is designed to be aero-dynamic. You'll also wear lightweight, treadless racing shoes—slippers, essentially—so walk carefully on the ice. Your gloves will be equipped with spikes on the fingertips and knuckles to help give you traction when you push. Finally, you'll have a helmet with a face shield. To prevent the face shield from fogging up, many riders smear it with shampoo.

2. Take a seat. When you emerge from the warming house at the top of the run, your coach will have your sled waiting at the start. It will have been weighed by officials, and the temperature of the steel runners checked to make sure they haven't been overheated. Sit down on the sled. Your butt should be in the center of the pod (the custom-molded seat of the sled), with your legs slightly bent and your feet tucked into the curve of the runners.

3. Take a mental run. At this point you have about 60 to 90 seconds to wait while the slider ahead of you completes his or her run; use the time to visualize yourself completing the course. Picture the turns and the line you will take through them. When it is your turn, you will be given a green light, at which point you'll have 30 seconds to start your run. This is when the face shield comes down.

4. Rock it. The start looks simple on TV, but it requires a complex series of moves and is the most critical part of the run—the only part in which you have direct control over your speed. USA Luge has built a 100-foot indoor start ramp at Lake Placid, and national team members spend hours practicing there year-round. Grab the handles, mounted in the ground on either side of the sled, and rock the sled back and forth to make sure it is in the groove and pointed straight.

> *Like sprinters dipping at the tape, sliders will often try to shave a few hundredths of a second at the finish by lifting themselves off the pod and sliding their feet out in front of the sled to trip the electric timer.*

FOR YOUR INFORMATION

5. Pull. This phase of the start is known as "the compression." After two or three rocks, drive the sled back as far as you can. Your arms should be straight out in front of you and you should be bent forward, completely between your knees.

6. Drive. At the maximum point of the compression, you'll feel a natural bounce. At that instant, pull back with your arms, back, and hips. As your upper body reaches vertical, release the handles.

For maximum speed, keep the sled in the track's center through the curves.

7. Paddle. Take three quick paddles along the ice with the spiked tips of your fingers. (Some sliders use their knuckles.)

8. Settle in. After the third paddle, reach down into the sled beside your hips, raise yourself up, and slide your butt down into the sled, against the crotch piece. At the same time, straighten your legs out between the runners. The sled will support your back and shoulders, but you will be holding your head up to see the track ahead of you.

9. Follow your line. You steer the sled by pushing down and in on one of the flexible runners, while pressing down into the sled with the opposite shoulder, essentially "scissoring" the sled. On any curve, a luge has a tendency to ride up the banking on the start, come down the banking in the middle, and then ride back up. For a fast run, you need to keep the sled running straight through the center of the turn. If done right, you'll feel what sliders call the "push," as the g-forces catch up with you coming out of the turn and accelerate you down the course.

10. Sit up. After the finish line, the track will slope up to help you stop. You should sit up, put your feet down on either side, and pull up on the front runners. You might also want to go "Wheeeee!"

MOTOCROSS

HOW TO PERFORM A MOTOCROSS BACKFLIP

"The minute I rode a dirt bike I knew someday someone would do a backflip," was how Caleb Wyatt put it in an interview with EXPN.com. Wyatt, of course, is a freestyle MotoX god, having become that someday someone—the first rider to complete a backflip on a full-size (125-cc or larger) bike. Wyatt, then a 26-year-old daredevil from Medford, Oregon, squared the big circle on April 25, 2002, becoming the Roger Bannister of the handlebar set, as he beat such better-known riders as Mike Metzger and Travis Pastrana to the punch. And, just as with the four-minute mile, once one athlete had broken the barrier, others quickly followed. Metzger, Pastrana, Corey Hart, all were soon pulling backflips—in competition, over rapidly widening gaps, with extra wrinkles like one-handed and "no-feet" maneuvers.

As with all extreme sports, video documentation is essential—and plentiful. Unlike in the stick-and-ball sports, there really are no scores or stats in many of the extreme disciplines; there's only the move. And these days, it seems, no huck or jump goes unrecorded. A quick scan of the Internet will turn up dozens of clips. There's Wyatt's historic flip, a grainy but still electrifying sequence. There's Metzger's double. Pastrana's one-hander. If seeing is believing, downloading is MotoX's best disciple.

There is also, it should be pointed out, a great deal of carnage on display. Anyone who forgets the physics involved in flipping motorbikes 90 feet through the air should check out some of the wipeouts that all the top riders have survived. All sports have their risks and all sports demand sacrifice, but MotoX riders tend to chart their progress in broken wrists, concussions, and the occasional shattered pelvis. Consider this matter-of-fact response by Metzger to a MotoX Web site's query about past injuries: "Broke back three times, both femurs, both arms several times & surgery on knees." Kinda puts that tennis elbow in perspective, doesn't it?

It also makes the constant advancement of skills and stunts all the more impressive. Fast-forward from Caleb Wyatt's first successful flip back in the dark ages of '02 to the 2004 Winter X Games in Aspen, Colorado. There, in front of a raucous crowd and live TV cameras, Wyatt took the Best Trick gold medal with a backflip over a 90-foot gap, during which he took first his feet off the bike, then his hands. Wyatt called the trick the Smirnoff Riot. We call it sick.

Who knows what's next for the MotoX gods. If you want to catch up, though, you better be ready to flip out.

---

1. Know your bike. The pros ride 250-cc models, which means you'll be sitting on about 200 pounds worth of motorcycle, with a two-stroke, five-speed engine. Some top riders practice their moves on smaller bikes, but the 250 will give you the power and pop you

Over the top: No matter how wide the gap or wild

need. Just remember: If you bail out, there's a lot of bike coming down with you.

2. Ramp it up. Wyatt pulled his first flip off a dirt mound, but most competitions take place on ramps. Study the shape and size carefully before you attempt a takeoff.

3. Throttle up. Take as long a run-up as you feel comfortable with. Accelerate all the way toward the ramp, but keep a light hand on the throttle. You should be up off the seat, your upper body straight, as the bike hits the ramp and the suspension compresses.

4. Gas off. As your front wheel passes the top end of

the trick, MotoX riders will find a way to pull it off.

the ramp, give it some throttle. This will lift the bike. You don't have to pull back on the handlebars too hard.

5. Don't look back. At least not too soon. Keep your head neutral as you rotate. Throwing it back can cause you to over-rotate.

6. Let the bike rotate. A proper takeoff will set the whole flip in motion. Trying to hurry it or jerk it around can cause you to wipe out. As the suspension bounces back, it will help keep the bike on course.

7. Spot the landing. Once you've rotated far enough, you should be able to see the ground and orient your-self for landing.

8. Land square. When you touch down, stay above the saddle and absorb the impact through your knees and thighs, as well as through your grip on the handlebars. Don't try to accelerate or turn until the bike is completely steady. And don't try to get off and walk until *you're* steady!

LEGENDARY SPORTS HEROES

At the 2004 Winter X Games in Aspen, MotoX star Brian Deegan took a spectacular spill while attempting a "Mulisha Twist" (a 360-degree twisting jump) over a 90-foot gap from an ice takeoff to an ice landing. Deegan fell from his bike at the peak of the jump, dropping 45 feet to the ice, where he suffered a broken femur and two broken wrists. Less than two weeks later, Deegan was itching to start riding again and was telling an interviewer, "I want people to see how gnarly our sport is, and the risks we take. I want people to think, 'Oh, that was gnarly!'"

HOW TO DO THE OLLIE

Carl Sandburg once wrote, "May all your children be acrobats." Were the great American poet working today, that line might well be, "May all your children be skateboarders." For so often these days it can seem that nearly every public space with more than 20 square feet of concrete is overrun with kids performing a rattling, dazzling collection of stunts, their wheeled boards seemingly exempt from the laws of gravity. New generations of skaters continually push the boundaries of what's possible, adding height, twists, or extra wrinkles to moves with names such as the Two-foot Nose 360 Shove-it, the 50/50 Saranwrap, or the Backside Crooked Grind.

> **TRAINING TIP**
>
> *When Rodney Muller started skating, his father, a doctor, made him wear so much protective gear that Rodney was nicknamed "The Human Pad."*

But even a sport as protean as skating has its fundamentals. Consider the ollie. Most skaters probably don't know that this most essential of skills was actually invented by a guy named—duh!—Ollie. Back in 1978, Alan "Ollie" Gelfand was a 15-year-old "skate rat" from Hollywood, Florida, and a member of the seminal group known as the Bones Brigade. Working the rough-surfaced concrete pool of a dilapidated skate park one day, Gelfand found that at the top of the bowl, his board would kick off the lip into the air and, after turning 180 degrees, come back to his legs. He found that by bending his knees, he could gain control of the board and ride it back down the bowl. "It was all by accident," Gelfand has said of the trick that he at first called the "no hands air," but that skaters quickly dubbed "the ollie."

By 1981, Gelfand had given up skating. (Injuries had slowed him down and, besides, he had gotten his driver's license and was already getting into racing cars.) It was about that time that another young Florida skater, Rodney Muller, took the ollie to flat ground and revolutionized street skating. "Every trick starts out as an ollie," says Grant Brittain of *Transworld Skateboarding* magazine. "Learn this trick first. Learn it and practice it all the time," is the advice of skateboard.com, a leading Web site of the sport.

So, before you head out to rock that Frontside No-Comply Varial, make sure you've got your ollie wired.

1. Get on board. Your back foot should be centered, with the ball of the foot almost back at the tail of the board. Position your front foot just ahead of the middle of the board (Fig. A).

2. Bend your knees. This is where your power and pop come from. Make sure your center of gravity is

FIG. A   FIG. B   FIG. C

over the center of the board. Extend your arms if you
need to maintain your balance.

3. Go ahead and jump. (By the way, forget that 44.5-
inch mark; when you're first attempting to ollie, don't
even try to go over anything. You just want to get off
the ground.) Make your jump off your back foot, driving
the tail of the board into the pavement (Fig. B). This
will drive the board into the air.

**4. Slide your front foot up the grip tape as the
board rises.** This will essentially drag the board higher
into the air (Fig. C) and also level the board at the
peak of the ollie (Fig. D), next page.

FIG. D   FIG. E   FIG. F

5. Prepare for landing. Extend your legs as you and the board drop to the pavement (Fig. E). Land flat on all four wheels, your feet positioned over the axles (Fig. F).

LEGENDARY SPORTS HEROES

When Ollie Gelfand was still the only skater performing the "air ollie," he repeatedly had his shoes stolen—by skeptical observers searching for Velcro patches or other devices—with which, they were convinced, he must be "grabbing" the board.

HOW TO SKI JUMP

Quick! Name the most famous ski jumper in the world. Unless you grew up in Finland or Japan or Eastern Europe—where such athletes are national heroes—you'll probably answer, "that *Wide World of Sports* guy." Vinko Bogataj is the Yugoslavian ski jumper whose spectacular rag-doll fall in the world ski flying championships played every Saturday afternoon for 25 years as the visual embodiment of the phrase "the agony of defeat" during the opening montage of *ABC's Wide World of Sports.* (Impossible as it may be to believe, Bogataj survived his wipeout with nothing worse than a concussion; he lives on in happy and healthy retirement as a cultural touchstone.)

To dedicated fans in countries around the world, ski jumping offers a thrilling blend of beauty and action. And to the athletes themselves, it seems, there is nothing quite like the feeling of powering down that hill and exploding into the air. As Alan Alborn, who in 2002 set the U.S. distance record of 221.5 meters, puts it in the U.S. Ski Team's media guide, "It's really like flying."

Ski jumpers compete on three categories of hill. The first, the normal hill, was originally called the 70-meter because that was the distance that most skiers would jump on such a hill. Nowadays the normal hill is called a 90-meter or sometimes the K90, since that's how far modern jumpers go. The large hill, once called the 90-meter, is now called the 120-meter. Then there are the flying hills, which range from 160-meter to 185-meter. There are only six ski-flying hills in the world, including Copper Peak in Ironwood, Minnesota, which has not been used since 1994. The record distance for a ski jump was set by Andi Goldberg of Austria—who, unlike the hapless Bogataj, experienced the thrill of victory as he soared 225 meters off a flying hill in Planica, Slovenia, in March 2000.

FOR THE RECORD *The first recorded North American ski jumping record was set in 1887 by one Mikkel Hemmestvedt, who soared a majestic 13 meters.*

For a thrill of your own, suit up and go ahead and jump.

1. Take it from the top. Poised at the top of the inrun—the 38-degree slope leading to the takeoff spot—you will be shown a flashing green light and will have 15 seconds to begin your jump. Generally, you'll want to wait for a hand signal from your coach or spotter, stationed down the hill near the takeoff point, giving you the sign that the wind is right for a jump.

2. Play the hunch. That is, hunch low over your skis as you go down the inrun. Your legs should be bent at about a 90-degree angle, shoulder width apart, with your skis (which are about 8 1/2 feet long) pointing straight ahead. Keep your chest flat against the tops of your thighs and your head up. Your arms should be held tight to your sides, with your hands pointing behind, palms up. Think of the fins on an old Cadillac. Speaking of which, during the inrun you will reach a speed of 55 to 60 mph.

3. Clear for takeoff. As you continue from the inrun down parallel grooves in the hill to the 11-degree slope of the takeoff point, you should be coiled and ready to spring. At the takeoff, explode out of your crouch, straightening your body out toward the tips of your skis, arms still tight to your sides.

Jan Stenerud, the Hall of Fame kicker for the Kansas City Chiefs, Green Bay Packers, and Minnesota Vikings, who was born in Norway, attended the University of Montana on a ski-jumping scholarship.

LEGENDARY SPORTS HEROES

4. Think "V" for victory. Introduced in the late 1980s, the V-technique, in which you push your skis into a "V" formation, with the front tips forming the open end, revolutionized the sport, allowing jumpers to fly far-ther than ever. Strive to remain level in the air, your body achieving maximum wind resistance toward the ground, while eliminating wind resistance forward. Throughout your flight you will be about 10 to 12 feet off the ground.

5. Mind your P's and K's. The landing area is bound by two control points. The first, the P-point, is the spot at which the hill is still at its steepest. The second, the K-point, marks where the hill starts to flatten out. You

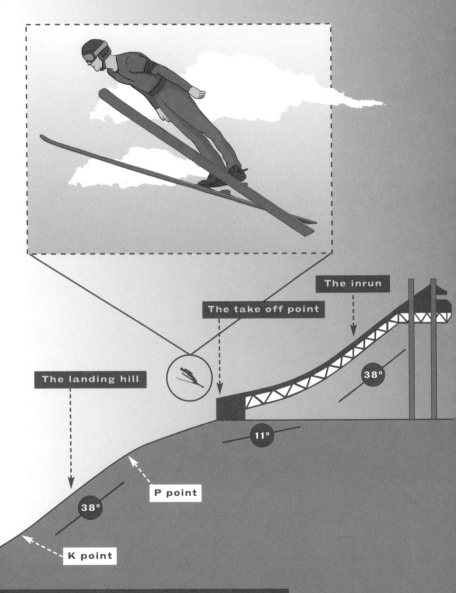

The inrun

The take off point

The landing hill

38°

11°

P point

38°

K point

The V-technique revolutionized the sport, giving jumpers more air time.

will want to land as far down the hill as possible while still maintaining form and safety.

6. "Mark" your landing. You must land with one foot in front of the other and bend forward as you land. This is known as a telemark landing. Your legs should absorb the impact, while your arms come up to maintain balance.

SURFING

HOW TO RIDE THE CURL AT JAWS

"Big wave, tiny man."

That's how Laird Hamilton puts it, and in those four simple words you have the essence of surfing at Jaws. Located on the north shore of Maui, Jaws is the ultimate big-wave break, a hellish convergence of ocean and reef where 60-foot, 10,000-ton walls of water—apartment-building-size hunks of the Pacific—come roaring in to crash against the lava cliffs. A spot that for years was believed to be unsurf-able. Laird Hamilton, on the other hand, is "little" only in comparison to such otherworldy monsters. In comparison to other surfers he is a giant, a legend, a god in a wetsuit. Six-foot-three, 225 pounds, bronzed and ripped and cover-boy handsome; California-born, Hawaii-raised, the son of 1960s surfing star Bill Hamilton; married to volleyball goddess Gabrielle Reese, Hamilton was once described in the pages of *Sports Illustrated* as "the Charles Atlas of surfing . . . a caricature of physical prodigy and alpha dog temperament."

Waves the size of those at Jaws (which, by the way, was given its name by sensationalist surf writers; the locals and the surfers call it Peahi) are moving too fast, at more than 35 mph, for a surfer to catch up and paddle into the swell. Hamilton and his buddies came up with the concept of tow-in surfing. Standing on his board, with his feet anchored in the sort of foot straps that windsurfers use, a surfer could hold onto a towrope attached to a Jet Ski and be pulled into the perfect spot in the wave, then let go for the ride of his life. The Jet Ski would also be there to rescue the surfer should the jaws of Peahi snap down on him. Working as a team, a pair of surfers could get in dozens of rides a day. Some purists yelped, decrying the use of artificial power, but the mind-blowing possibilities opened up by tow-in surfing proved irresistible. After all, however you are delivered to the wave, you're still alone out there on that god-awful mountain of water.

Before you gas up the Jet Ski and wax up your board, however, you'll want to check on the conditions. Most of the year Jaws is actually pretty tame, but on 10 or 15 days a year, when the wind is running right, Jaws rears up and asserts itself. Surfers the world over monitor conditions and wave heights over the Internet, and when the magic is right, the hardiest make the scene. Here's how to be one of them.

1. Pick your board. In the old days, when paddling fast was the only way to get onto big waves (we're only talking 20- and 25-footers here), you needed long, fast, streamlined boards. But at more than 10 feet long and 25 pounds, those boards were unwieldy. Today, with the advent of the tow-in, you'll be riding a board about 7 feet long and 15 inches wide. (Hamilton has been known to use one as short as 6´2˝. On a board like that, you'll be able to carve the wave, not just ride it.)

2. Get a tow hold. Lie back on the deck of your board, grasp hold of the towrope attached to the back of the personal watercraft (a Jet Ski, Wave Runner, or some other similar vehicle).

3. Get a toe hold. When you feel the board start to plane across the water, slip your feet into the toe straps mounted on the board and stand up. The toe straps help keep your feet on the board even at the tremendous speeds generated by a 60-footer. Unless you're riding "goofy," you'll have your left foot forward, at about the center of your board, and your right foot back, over the fins. Stand with your legs straight, leaning back to keep the rope taut, feeling the pull in your legs and back. As the PWC builds speed, up to 25 to 30 mph, you'll feel the bounce and chop under the board.

4. Head for the wave. Far out from shore, the buildup of the wave will be subtle. The driver of the PWC will tow you almost parallel to the developing trough and then, when you've exchanged signals indicating that this is the wave you intend to ride, he'll carve a quick hairpin turn. It's time for the moment of truth.

The tow-in technique has delivered surfers into the jaws of monsters.

5. Whip it. Leaning back against the rope, turn hard away from the wake of the PWC and onto the swell. Lean hard through the turn. You will accelerate strongly at this point.

6. Toss it. Drop the rope and let yourself ride up into the shoulder of the wave. Now drop down the face and race the curl. When (if?) you come out the other end, thank the gods of Peahi—including Laird Hamilton— for the thrill. And for making it alive.

FURTHER READING

BASEBALL
Coaching Baseball: Skills and Drills
By Brad A. Stockton • Coaches Choice Books, 263 pages
The late Stockton, who coached at the University of Houston, was one of the game's foremost teachers. His instruction is clear, accessible and timeless.

Ball Four
By Jim Bouton • Wiley, 465 pages
Bouton's classic account of his 1969 season pitching for the Seattle Pilots and the Houston Astros revolutionized sportswriting; it also captures the quirky essence of the knuckle ball.

BASKETBALL
A Sense of Where You Are
By John McPhee • Farrar, Straus and Giroux, 144 pages
McPhee's first book, analyzing the play of a young Bill Bradley, and still one of the best inside views of any sport ever written.

BOWLING
Bowling: How to Master the Game
By Parker Bohn III • Universe Publishing, 160 pages
The 1999 PBA Player of the Year covers the sport, from equipment to tournament strategies in a handsome book that includes computer-generated lane diagrams.

BOXING
Cut Time: An Education at the Fights
By Carlo Rotella • Houghton Mifflin, 222 pages
Rotella is an English professor, not a fighter, but his marvelously written essays capture the essence of what goes on inside the ropes.

FIGURE SKATING
Figure Skating Champions
By Steve Milton and Gerard Chataigneau • Firefly Books Ltd., 32 pages
This slim book is short on instruction, but, with wonderful photos of the most dynamic modern skaters in action, it is long on inspiration.

FOOTBALL
Play Football the NFL Way: Position-by-Position Techniques and Drills for Offense, Defense and Special Teams
By Tom Bass • St. Martin's Griffin, 413 pages
With the NFL's stamp of approval, this linebacker-sized tome covers the game, complete with diagrams and a comprehensive glossary.

GOLF
Ben Hogan's Five Lessons: The Modern Fundamentals of Golf
Simon and Schuster, 127 pages
This book, first published in 1957, and illustrated with elegant drawings by Anthony Ravielli, is like getting a personal lesson from one of the game's all-time greats.

Harvey Penick's Little Red Book: Lessons and teachings from a Lifetime in Golf
By Harvey Penick with Bud Shrake • Simon and Schuster, 175 pages
The timeless classic, written when Penick was 81 and, indeed, had a lifetime of golfing wisdom to share.

GYMNASTICS
Men's Gymnastics Coaching Manual
By Lloyd Readhead • Trafalgar Square Publishing, 208 pages
This far-from-flashy nuts-and-bolts primer from the British Gymnastics Association presents the skills of men's gymnastics in a clear, unintimidating fashion.

Kurt Thomas on Gymnastics
By Kurt Thomas • Fireside, 223 pages
The father of the Flair introduces the reader to the sport that made him famous and does it with flair.

HOCKEY
Complete Hockey Instruction: Skills and Strategies for Coaches and Players
By Dave Chambers • Contemporary Books, 283 pages
The definitive resource for anyone seeking to learn the game.

Open Net
By George Plimpton • The Lyons Press, 256 pages
Plimpton's account of playing goal in preseason camp with the 1977 New York Rangers is fascinating and often hilarious, and gives a vivid idea of what it's like to face an NHL attacker.

HORSE RACING
The Perfect Ride
By Gary Stevens • Citadel Press, 236 pages
One of the greatest jockeys ever, Stevens takes the reader inside the racing world, from the jockeys' changing room to the stretch run of the Derby.

NASCAR RACING
Stock Car Driving Techniques
By Don Alexander • MBI Publishing, 191 pages
With commentary by the likes of Jeff Gordon and Terry Labonte, race school instructor Alexander's book is as informative—if not as loud—as a lapping session at Daytona.

SKATEBOARDING
Hawk—Occupation: Skateboarder
By Tony Hawk • Regan Books, 307 pages
Du-uh! It's Tony Hawk.

SKI JUMPING
The History of Ski Jumping
By Tim Ashburner • Quiller Press, 128 pages
This lovingly compiled and generously illustrated work covers the history and development of the sport from the 19th century through the 2002 Winter Olympics.

SOCCER
How to Play the Game: The Official Playing and Coaching Manual of the United States Soccer Federation
Universe, 320 pages
An impressively comprehensive work, supplemented throughout by easy-to-understand diagrams.

SURFING
The Encyclopedia of Surfing
By Matt Warshaw • Harcourt Inc., 774 pages
Dude! The former editor of Surfer magazine covers the sport from A to Z.

Pipe Dreams: A Surfer's Journey
By Kelly Slater with Jason Borte • Reagan Books, 338 pages
This well-illustrated memoir by the six-time world champ is not a how-to, but it does take the reader along for the big-wave ride.

TABLE TENNIS
Winning Table Tennis
By Dan Seemiller and Mark Holowchak • Human Kinetics, 177 pages
From the handshake grip to elite tournament tactics, many-time national champ Seemiller serves up a clear, readable introduction to a sport far more sophisticated than most basement players can imagine.

TENNIS
Maximum Tennis
By Nick Saviano • Human Kinetics, 195 pages
Saviano, the director of coaching for the USTA, offers a clear and inspiring introduction to the skills and strategies of the game.

TRACK & FIELD
Track and Field Omnibook
By Ken Doherty • Tafnews, 514 pages
This out-of-print volume remains the most comprehensive introduction to the techniques of the sport.

POLE VAULT
By Frank Ryan • Viking Press, 47 pages
Though innovations in technique and advances in technology are throwing vaulters ever higher, Ryan's book remains the definitive guide for athletes in the sport's most dynamic event.

ACKNOWLEDGMENTS

A little knowledge is a dangerous thing, especially for the author of a how-to book, who had better have a lot of knowledge—or know where to get it. This book would not have been possible without the input and guidance of a number of friends and colleagues, whose knowledge (far more than a little in every case) helped to illuminate the wide world of sports skills and techniques. A tip of the cap (or helmet or visor or sweatband, as the case may be) to Lars Anderson, Mark Beech, Steve Cannella, Brian Cazeneuve, Richard Deitsch, Jaime Diaz, Richard Hoffer, Jack McCallum, Merrell Noden, Jeff Pearlman, Pat Putnam, Steve Rushin, Carl Weingarten and Jon Wertheim. A cheer, too, to the staff of the *Sports Illustrated* research library, a treasure trove of sports resources.

Thanks to Reid Boates and Rob Fleder for their advice, to Dick Preston for his writerly encouragement and to Lolly—as always—for everything. Finally, I am especially grateful to Jason Rekulak for his encouragement, his deft editorial touch, and his hall-of-fame patience.